SPECIAL PawPrint

A DOG'S BRAIN

How Canines Think, Feel and Learn

Contents

32

58

84

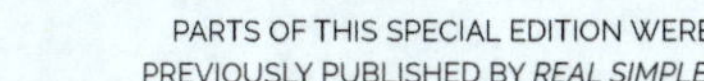

PARTS OF THIS SPECIAL EDITION WERE PREVIOUSLY PUBLISHED BY *REAL SIMPLE*.

INTRODUCTION

Evolutionary Ideas

The dog's journey from wilderness to our living rooms is thanks to the canine mind's powerful ability to adapt

BY COURTNEY MIFSUD

THE WORK OF A Russian geneticist is perhaps most responsible for science's understanding of the process by which wolves were domesticated into the friendly canine companions known today. By the early 1950s the U.S.S.R., led by the country's dictator, had essentially banned the study of genetics and sought to discredit genetic principles. Having been fired by Moscow's Central Research Laboratory of Fur Breeding, a Russian geneticist named Dmitry K. Belyaev began a remarkable experiment at an animal research facility in Siberia. Belyaev set about trying to trace the evolutionary pathway of domesticated animals, focusing on silver-back foxes, a melanistic version of the red fox that had been bred in farms for their glossy black fur.

Over the next 40 years, Belyaev sought to selectively breed foxes for tameness around humans in an effort to create a strain of captive foxes that would be easier to work with. In the beginning, very few foxes met Belyaev's strict criteria for friendliness, but by the 10th generation 20% of the foxes were tame. And after 40 generations, 80% of the young foxes fit his friendliness-to-humans criteria. The domesticated foxes were more eager to hang out with humans, whimpered to attract attention and sniffed and licked their caretakers. They wagged their tails when they were happy or excited, while the wild cubs hid in the corner or made aggressive noises toward the researchers.

Part of Belyaev's hypothesis was that tameness was the critical factor in natural selection for the domestication of animals. Across a wide spectrum of species, domesticated animals seem to share traits that differ from their wild counterparts: their body size shifts, the fur color changes and the timing of their reproductive cycle may be altered. More specifically, their fur becomes

Wolves and dogs can look quite similar, but actually the two species have diverged considerably over the past tens of thousands of years. The neuroanatomy of dogs has adapted in profound ways to aid domestication.

curly or wavy, they have shortened or curly tails and they develop floppy ears. Darwin noted, in *On the Origin of Species*, that "not a single domestic animal can be named which has not, in some country, drooping ears." With the exception of elephants, drooping ears do not ever occur in the wild.

In less than a decade, some of Belyaev's domesticated foxes had floppy ears and curly tails. Over generations their adrenal glands became smaller and smaller, lessening the stress hormone levels in tame foxes compared with wild ones. Serotonin levels also increased, producing "happier" cubs. Over the course of the experiment, the research team also found the domesticated foxes developed "muttlike" fur patterns, and they had shorter, rounder, more doglike snouts and chunkier, rather than gracile, limbs. The tame foxes developed longer reproductive periods than their wild counterparts. They also lost their "musky fox smell." Another change associated with selection for tameness is that the domesticated foxes, unlike wild foxes, are capable of following the gaze of a human as well as dogs do. By selecting for a single behavioral trait, and allowing only the foxes with the strongest human connection to breed, Belyaev's experiment helped demonstrate that all of the anatomical and physiological changes that came with natural selection and domestication were ultimately linked to an animal's willingness to bond with humans.

Decades have passed since Belyaev began his silver fox breeding program, and domestic foxes are far from the domestic dogs gracing our homes, but insight into their evolutionary journey helps to shape our understanding of the ancient connection between humans and our favorite companions.

Although Dmitry Belyaev, pictured here, died in 1985, the silver fox domestication experiment continues to this day. Led by Lyudmila Trut, a team of Russian geneticists recently identified key chromosomes for these changes.

FOXES AND DOGS ARE CLOSE cousins who diverged from one another along the wolf lineage about 12 million years ago. Wolves are only separated from dogs by tens of thousands of years. Pooches still retain many of wolves' ancestral behaviors, but how many "doglike" tendencies are found among modern wolves? Research published by Eötvös Loránd University in Budapest showed that wolf puppies that were raised by humans could display affection and attachment toward their owners, feelings that lasted well into adulthood. Published in 2017, the study also showed that the thoroughly socialized wolves were remarkably more comfortable around new humans than their wild counterparts, even if the wolves sometimes exhibited a bit of fear. This research points to behaviors that may have led their ancestral wolf brethren to seek out comfort among humans, which could have sparked the evolutionary divergence to the hyper-cuddly furball known as man's best friend.

Dogs and wolves are very different species despite physical similarities and exhibit profoundly different traits and behaviors. Dogs have a natural affinity toward humans, with neurological research showing that they are happier with people than even members of their own species. Domestication has reinforced that dogs can find comfort in humans when stressed. However, even though the socialized wolves are better around

The Ismaili family in Macedonia shares their home with six wolves. Wolves raised in home environments can become incredibly friendly but often have deeply rooted social challenges that separate them from dogs.

people than wild wolves, they still display more wariness of humans than dogs display. Plus, the socialized wolves are more independent than dogs. Wolf pups are often literally lone wolves, left alone while the pack goes out to hunt and cultivating an intense level of self-sufficiency that dogs do not have.

Despite these differences, researchers have also found behavioral similarities. Wolves like to lick each other's faces as a greeting. They understand gestures like finger pointing and can also hold a person's gaze. Dorottya Ujfalussy, who led the study in Budapest, sought to learn more about the kinds of relationships that socialized wolves have with their human caregivers, with the goal of unpacking what makes dogs unique in their relationships with people and where those traits might have originated.

Throughout the study, Ujfalussy's team conducted experiments using wolf puppies that were raised by humans. These wolves came from the Family Dog Project, an initiative founded in 1994 by József Topál to study aspects of the dog-human relationship. For the purposes of this study, participants with the Family Dog Project were asked to raise wolf puppies through daily walks on leashes, cuddling, grooming and so on. The intense socialization of wolves in this study made them ideal subjects to reveal any differences that were innate or inborn.

As the wolf pups reached certain age milestones, the researchers visited the wolves and their foster families and conducted socialization tests to measure how attached the pups were to the humans with whom they lived. The researchers measured greetings displayed by the wolves to four different types of human visitors—those that raised them, those that were around a lot, people they had met just once and people they had never met—at three age points, 6, 12 and 24 months. In the first of the experiments, the pups were exposed to the humans while among other wolves, giving them a security blanket of sorts. In the second, the pups met the humans on their own.

The researchers report that in all cases the 6-month-old pups greeted all humans warmly and affectionately. The 12- and 24-month-olds cheerily greeted humans they knew well but were slightly more

Researchers have found that breeding has reordered dogs' brains to outperform in certain areas. Highly skilled German shepherds have certain neurological differences that make the breed ideal for police work.

reserved with humans they didn't know or barely knew. They also noted that some of the the 12- and 24-month-old wolf pups showed crouching and tail-tucking when confronted with strangers, a sign of fear in wolves. The researchers note that because some of the wolves were 2 years old, it seemed reasonable to conclude that the attachment they felt and the affection they showed to those humans they knew well likely would continue into adulthood.

TAMENESS MIGHT SUGGEST WHY wolves were first bred to become dogs, but what role did specialized tasks, such as herding sheep or pointing to prey, play in the evolution of dogs? Many of these behaviors are closely linked to specific breeds—German shepherds are preferred for police work, while beagles have superior snouts for following a scent. A recent study shed light on how the canine brain might have evolved in response to natural selection's pressure on certain behaviors.

Erin Hecht, an assistant professor in the department of human evolutionary biology at Harvard University, examined the MRI scans of dogs from unique breeds to discern if a breed's specialized behavioral adaptations and abilities might present as neuroanatomical changes. When she compared the scans of 62 purebred pet dogs across 33 unique breeds, she did notice patterns in the differences. In other words, the specialized behavioral adaptations of a dog's breed were clearly visible as neuroanatomical changes. Hecht discovered six networks of brain regions that change together, each associated with breeding for a specific trait or behavior, such as guarding, companionship, or sight and scent hunting. For example, in dogs that hunt by sight, she found differences in a region of the brain involved in eye movement and spatial navigation. "We think that might be related to visually tracking a bird or whatever the hound is following," Hecht told *Harvard Magazine* in 2020.

Hecht and her team published the findings in the *Journal of Neuroscience* in 2019 and presented a phylogenetic analysis of the family tree of modern dog breeds. That research showed that the differences in brain structure present among breeds could not be explained by the deep ancestry associated with domestication thousands of years ago. Instead, Hecht found that the selection pressure for specific behaviors among the separate branches of the tree likely occurred within the past 200 years. That selection pressure led to the simultaneous emergence of certain networks of brain structures, so sight dogs from different branches of the family tree shared similar anatomical variances.

Since 1959, Dmitry Belyaev's fox studies in Siberia have become so well-known that they have inspired Hecht to begin studying the evolution of the canine brains. The offspring of the tamest foxes from Belyaev's experiment are still being studied in Novosibirsk, Siberia, to further investigate the link between the selection for tameness and physical traits such as wavy hair and floppy ears. In the nearly six decades since the experiments began, little work has been done to investigate changes in the foxes' brains. Hecht and Christina Rogers Flattery, a postdoctoral fellow in Hecht's lab, are working on that now. Having established through their study on dog breeds that changes in behavior are linked to changes in neuroanatomy, the Hecht lab has begun examining the brains of these tame foxes to see what the selection pressure exerted by humans decades ago on a canine looks like. "The brain regions we see implicated in this selection for tameness are in the limbic system and the prefrontal cortex," Hecht said. "The limbic system governs instinctual emotional reactions, the fight-or-flight response and aspects of social behavior that are cued by scents, while the prefrontal cortex regulates volitional types of behavior as well as more complex aspects of social behavior, like interpreting social signals and deciding what types of social signals to send in return. That's where we're seeing changes so far in the foxes."

Hecht is interested in what these studies might reveal about the brain's plasticity, meaning how do innate adaptations interact with lived experience to shape and change neuroanatomy. "We know that training is doing something," said Hecht. "We're trying to figure out how far an innate genetic inheritance gets you. And then, what's the additional bump that you'd get from experience and learning?" The researchers plan to establish the dog as a model for studying how structures within the brain evolve over time, and how the brain balances the innate with what can be changed. "I believe a lot of questions can be answered with these animals," says Sophie Barton, a third-year PhD candidate in Hecht's lab, "because we know what selection pressures they underwent to develop various skills and different behaviors."

Ultimately, the story of how the canine brain developed is also a story of the minds of humankind at the time. If humans and wolves had not come to an understanding tens of thousands of years ago, the tameness and friendliness that separates Fido from his fanged cousins might not have developed. The changes that the canine brain has endured over the years has laid the groundwork for a bond that transcends other species. (The phrase man's best friend developed for a reason.) Humans have played a decisive role in the evolution of dogs, and these wolf descendants have worked their way into our hearts and been woven into the fabric of human society.

Floppy ears are one of the distinguishable traits that came from domestication.

Chapter One

THE CANINE BRAIN

Can an old dog learn new tricks? Who's a Good Boy Hunting? *Researchers are answering these and many other questions of intelligence*

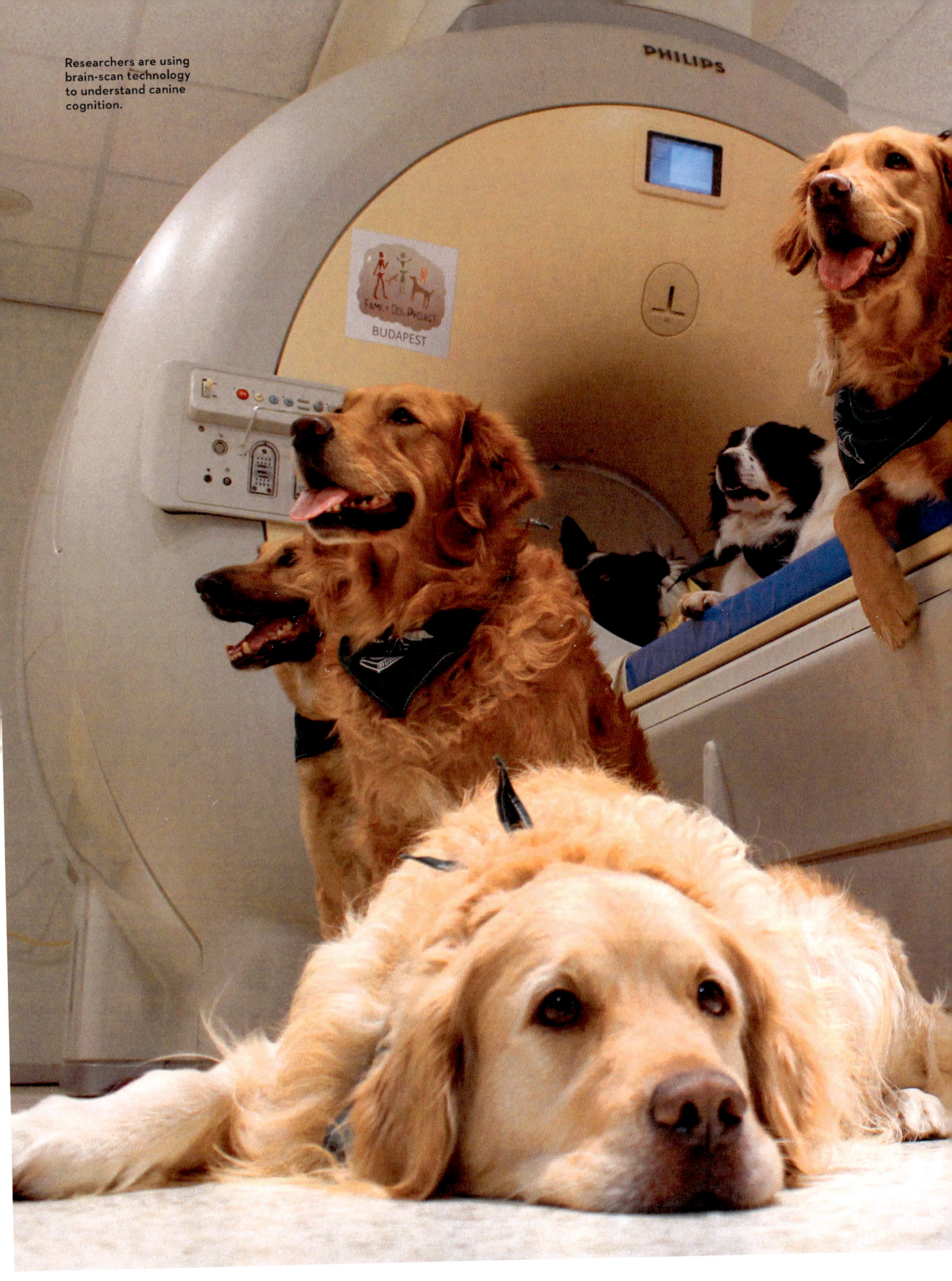

Researchers are using brain-scan technology to understand canine cognition.

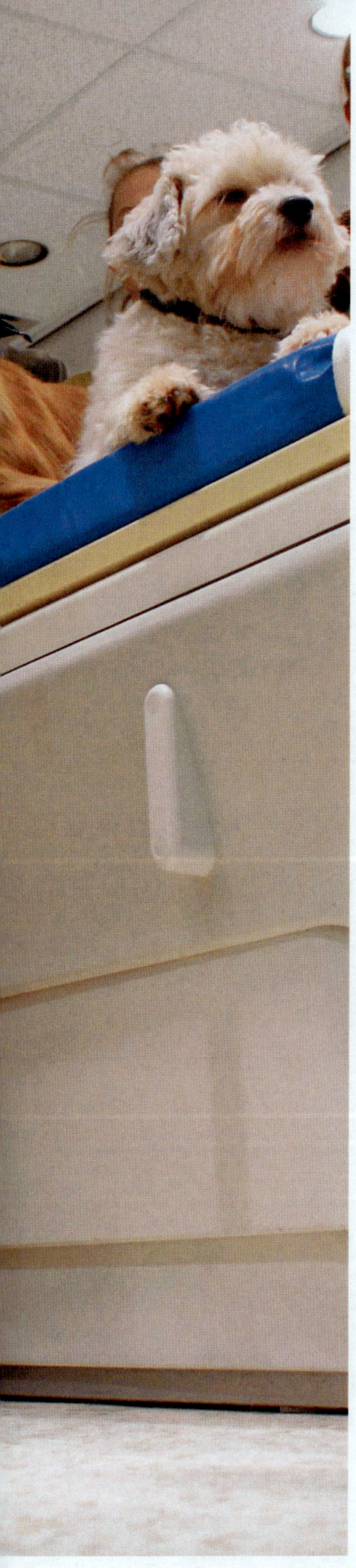

What Does a Dog Know?

Research reveals that the true genius of dogs lies in how they connect with us

BY DAVID BJERKLIE AND KATHRYN SATTERFIELD

ARNESSING THE POWER OF PEOPLE and their pups in the interest of science just seemed like, well, a stroke of genius. Enter the Genius Dog Challenge, an online campaign designed to raise awareness about research being done at Eötvös Loránd University (ELTE) in Budapest. Researchers there launched the world's first live-broadcast canine "tests" in 2020. They hoped to find more talented dogs to recruit for their study.

The Genius Dog Challenge featured six dogs, hailing from Spain, Hungary, Brazil, Norway, the Netherlands and the United States, who were part of a larger study. Their mission, explains lead scientist Claudia Fugazza, was to see how quickly they could learn the names of unfamiliar objects. All six learned quickly and easily. "We wanted to understand what [sets apart] these dogs that are so talented and so different from the other dogs," says Fugazza. The number of "gifted word learners" has now risen to 20, thanks to the publicity.

At first, the research team assumed younger dogs would have an advantage over their elders. "We expected puppies to learn at a faster rate because of their neuroplasticity," Fugazza says, but that was not the case. The researchers found that age didn't predict success or failure; still, only seven adult dogs showed an exceptional capacity for learning.

Most of the "gifted" dogs are Border collies, but the researchers are quick

While all animals have a natural tendency to categorize objects to some degree, "smarter" dogs can identify items by color or other markers.

to note that smarts are not unique to this breed. (There are reports of mutts excelling as well.) When they were narrowing the playing field, Fugazza says, 18 Border collies were among those that didn't rise to the top.

During the first phase of the challenge, researchers broadcast some of the tests they were performing for the larger study. They asked the owners of Rico, Whisky, Max, Squall, Gaia and Nalani to send the dogs into another room to fetch a specific toy from a group of many. This was repeated six times. After spending just one week learning the names of the toys, four of the dogs retrieved all objects. Their secret to success? The owners reported that simply playing with the dogs was all that was required. "What is most surprising is that these dogs appear to learn without training, just [through] daily interactions in a typical human family," Fugazza says.

Like the others, Whisky came ready to play. The eager Border collie would go into a different room to fetch the toy that her humans requested. For a different study, published in the journal *Scientific Reports* in February 2020, Whisky had 10 balls, seven rings, four ropes and four frisbees. Whisky became adept at finding specific toys within a category: fetching the "small Frisbee," and "multicolored ball," while the other Frisbees and balls remained untouched. Many animals have a natural sense of categorization to some degree, in order to "not waste energy or opportunities," notes Fugazza, "but the difference here is that these dogs may be able to learn a category which has a name, in a more humanlike way."

Livestreamed on YouTube and Facebook on Wednesdays through

December 2020, the "contests" earned real-time raves from viewers. During the finals, owners asked the canine contestants to fetch 12 toys over 12 different trips. Three dogs retrieved all 12 from a roomful of toys; one retrieved 11; and two found 10. The dogs always went into the toy room alone to ensure they couldn't be guided by inadvertent cues. Some would look around for a few seconds, nosing a few toys out of the way to select the one that had been named. On more than one occasion, a dog would self-correct, dropping the wrong toy in favor of the right one, before returning to the other room.

As for what separates gifted learners from the rest of the pack, that's a hard call. "At the moment we haven't found anything that is different, apart from the unbelievable capacity to rapidly learn new words," says Fugazza, who hopes that word-learning dogs can provide an animal model for studying exceptional performance.

The Brains Behind the Bark

The case for canine intelligence has never been stronger. And yet it can seem like people still fall into two camps: those who believe that dogs possess a unique intelligence we are just beginning to understand; and those who believe that dogs, as loyal and lovable as they are, have quite unexceptional minds, but fool us into thinking otherwise by being so well adapted to extracting treats from their owners.

Not exactly the Hatfields and the McCoys, but different views nonetheless. Maybe we shouldn't be surprised. Human beings, after all, have had a long and complicated relationship with animals. As Hal Herzog, a leading authority on human-animal interactions, memorably phrased it, "Some we love, some we hate and some we eat."

We pass judgment on animals, at least in part, based on how smart and self-aware we believe they are. The 2,500-year-old stories we refer to as Aesop's Fables bestowed rich inner lives on the animals that served up lessons in those tales. And yet in 1641, Descartes could confidently declare that animals "eat without pleasure; cry without pain; grow without knowing it. They desire nothing, fear nothing, know nothing." Two centuries later, on the other hand, Charles Darwin argued that a study of the animal world, humans included, revealed not only physiological similarities, but psychological ones as well.

Scientists in the 20th century sought to put a finer point on the matter. Much of the research since has been focused on primates (and rats, of course), but scrutiny has also been trained on dolphins, pigeons, parrots, crows, even the octopus, which, in the view of some scientists, may have been the first intelligent being on the planet. Scientists have spent hundreds of thousands of research hours in the field, patiently observing animals in their native habitats, but they've easily spent more than 10 times that effort in labs, devising experiments to test memory, attention, learning and communication.

Researchers have also grimly extracted and measured countless brains. "How big a brain does the animal have?" is still a reflexive question, but according to neuroscientist Gregory Berns of Emory University, in Atlanta, we've come to understand that "it's really about how the parts of the brain talk to each other." Berns, author of the best-selling books *How Dogs Love Us* and *What It's Like to Be a Dog*, has pioneered the use of MRI technology to peer into the brains of dogs. By harnessing this powerful tool, his team has been able to track how dogs recognize humans, how they distinguish voices and words, even how they experience jealousy.

> **"Dr. Berns's team has been able to track how dogs recognize humans, how they distinguish voices and words, even how they experience jealousy.**

Where scientists once saw the study of domestic dogs as hopelessly tainted by their relationship with us, scientists now see this dog-human relationship as the *focus* of their research. In the past 25 years, research centers devoted to dog cognition and the human-dog relationship have been established around the world, and for more than a decade the Canine Science Forum has attracted thousands of researchers in various specialties every two years. In July 2021, a virtual version of the conference covered topics ranging from "Comparing Human-Directed Communicative Abilities of Juvenile Companion Dogs and Miniature Pigs" to "Dog-Human Eye Contact: The Connection with Head Shape, Breed Function and Age."

Despite the growing research, many misconceptions about canine intelligence persist. "One that always comes to my mind," says Berns, "is that all dogs are the same. But in fact, everything that we and other researchers have found has shown that dogs are individuals. They're as different from each other as we are from each other." Canine intelligence is also not something a dog simply has either more or less of. Rather, as Duke University's Brian Hare, professor of evolutionary anthropology, points out, "There are different types of intelligence. Different dogs are good at different things." We can see variability among breeds, but also within a given breed. Individual dogs can have different competencies in communication skills, working memory and self-control, as well as different levels of emotional intelligence.

Hare co-founded a company that helps owners assess their dog's unique smarts. Called Dognition, the company has a website that features interactive science-based games designed to measure five core dimensions of a dog's cognition: empathy, communication, cunning, memory and reasoning. After playing up to 20 games, each dog receives a profile report. (There are nine profiles in all.) A dog that scores as an "Ace" is "an accomplished problem solver with great communication skills." Ten percent of dogs fall into this category, but just 3% of participants earn Einstein status; they show the ability to "make inferences" and have an "excellent comprehension of the physical world." The language of the diplomas may raise an eyebrow, but it's hard to argue with the fun or the enthusiasm.

Individual differences notwithstanding, the true genius of dogs as a species, according to Hare, is their capacity to read and respond to an entire range of human communication, from body language, pointing fingers and other gestures to tone of voice, facial expressions, even words. It is easy for us to take this comprehension for granted, but it is this that allows them to be both companions and partners. We have come from a place where we once asked, How smart are dogs? to a place where we now ask, How are dogs smart?

It is no surprise, though, that it is this ability of dogs to read humans so well that causes most dog lovers to overestimate their dog's intelligence or understanding of the world. Dog lovers tend to believe they "just know" that their dog is intuiting human moods and intentions. Or that they understand how the human world works. How else to explain the Lassie-like anecdotes nearly every dog lover has at the ready? Or forget heroics, how else to explain a dog that masters deceit and deception or just plain mischief?

> **"Dogs are individuals. They're as different from each other as we are from each other."**
>
> —DR. GREGORY BERNS

Arizona State University dog researcher Clive Wynne poured a bit of cold water on canine intelligence claims in a 2016 special edition of *Current Directions in Psychological Science* devoted to dog cognition. "There can be little argument that dogs are remarkable beings: Their ability to inveigle a larger, stronger, and surely more intelligent species to support their welfare is itself striking enough," wrote Wynne. But just because dogs are incredibly skilled when it comes to social interactions with humans doesn't necessarily mean that they have more advanced cognitive abilities than other animals do. The dog's vaunted ability to follow our pointing finger, for example, is not entirely unique, notes Wynne: "It's simply day-to-day experience with humans using their limbs to deliver things that matter." Let's not kid ourselves, he suggests.

That doesn't mean, however, that we shouldn't give our dogs their due. Studies have shown that dogs have a solid understanding of object permanence. When a dog watches an object being placed in one of several containers and is then allowed to look for it, the dog knows which container to investigate first. That seems easy. But how about when a toy is placed in a container, the container is moved behind a screen, and then brought back out empty? Some dogs still seem to follow the chain of events, surmising that if they peek behind the screen, they will probably find the toy.

Other studies have found that dogs also seem to understand the permanence of an object's characteristics. When a dog biscuit is shown to a dog and then hidden from view momentarily, a dog will stare if the biscuit brought back into view has been swapped for a larger or smaller version. A dog will react in the same way if a yellow ball comes back a different color.

Dogs also appear to be better

Dr. Gregory Berns has trained more than 100 dogs to sit unrestrained in an MRI machine. He believes that if dogs were trained for awake-MRI tests (typically dogs are put under general anesthesia for an MRI), veterinarians could change the way cancer is treated.

Bastian, a rescue dog who lives with owner Joelle Andres in New York City, knows 51 words and supposedly "talks" to Andres using a soundboard with buttons for words such as "treat."

than little kids at learning to ignore bad instructions. Researchers set up an experiment in which dogs and tots were given a box and taught to turn a lever to open the lid and get a treat. When the lever was altered so it was no longer needed to open the box, the dogs learned to ignore the useless step and went directly for the treat, while the tots stuck to the original routine of using the lever.

Communicating Canines

On TikTok, Instagram and Facebook, clips of dogs "talking" have attracted hundreds of thousands of likes and followers. In 2019, colleagues of Federico Rossano, professor of cognitive science at the University of California, San Diego, began forwarding him clips of Christina Hunger, a speech and language pathologist who had taught her dog, Stella, to use word buttons to communicate. He was charmed but skeptical.

"We know they can learn because we know you can train pretty much any animal to learn a lot of things," says Rossano, who has worked extensively with chimpanzees, bonobos, marmosets, goats and horses, among other animals, including dogs. But he also knew that the humans behind the clips could be "cherry picking" them for success or could be cueing the dogs with body language and facial expressions. "If all you see is those clips, I would be the first to say : it's just clips."

But in 2020, after being contacted by Leo Trottier, a former graduate student in cognitive science who had designed a soundboard with word buttons for dogs, Rossano co-launched a study that includes 3,500 participants in 45 countries; most are canines, but there are a few hundred cats, as well as some horses and pigs. Besides filling out questionnaires and surveys regularly, the participants use video cameras to record the soundboard and to record humans any time they are interacting with the animals.

One of the fundamental claims, in terms of language or linguistic evolution, explains Rossano, "is that only humans have syntax, only humans are able to combine different concepts in ways that allow you to communicate more complex thoughts." And that, ultimately, is what language is. "There's been a long effort to show that different animals can [do that]. But there's really little evidence. It's not very convincing."

For Rossano, then, while there was reason to be cautious, there were also reasons to be intrigued. "Imagine a child. The child first produces one word, and then starts to combine two things. And then adds more words to describe what he or she is seeing in the world. We see dogs combining words, but the question is, do they only reproduce what is trained, or can they reproduce language flexibly?" As the study has progressed, so has the content of the "conversations" between some dogs and their humans. Initially the communication was largely an exchange of requests. But now, according to Rossano, "[We're seeing] a lot of commenting on humans' facial expressions or emotional displays."

This is very much in line with the findings of Emory neuroscientist Berns. "One of the things we [first looked at] many years ago in our [MRI] brain-imaging studies was the question, Do dogs have dedicated parts of their brain to process faces? Because primates do. And as we know, facial expressions are very important for primates." Berns identified the face-processing areas by showing pictures to the dogs while they were in the MRI scanner and comparing their reactions to pictures of faces, objects and nature scenes.

It makes sense that dogs share this special cognitive ability of eye-to-eye communication with humans. And certainly it plays a key role in the dog-human bond. "We know dogs care for humans," says Rossano, but we don't know "to what degree they're trying to understand what's going on, or just being a little manipulative, like, 'Oh, I see you're smiling, you're in a good mood . . . Want to go outside?'"

Intentions aside, dogs and humans are clearly attached by more than just a retractable leash. Scientists at Portsmouth University's Dog Cognition Centre, in the U.K., have found that dogs produce far more facial expressions when a human is watching them. And Japanese researchers have determined that dogs who gazed at their owners for an extended period of time experienced elevated levels of oxytocin, a hormone produced in the brain that is associated with nurturing and attachment. In response to this eye contact, the owners' levels of oxytocin increased too, which in turn help elicit the rewards of affection, including more eye contact.

Humans find it easy (if not automatic) to imagine an individual awareness in a beloved dog, an awareness that extends to us. But how sophisticated is that awareness? To what extent can our dogs put themselves in our shoes and view the world through our eyes? We refer to that capacity as having "a theory of mind," but according to Berns, that's likely a misnomer. "It takes a lot of neural hardware to do [that]," says Berns, "so it's unlikely that other animals have that ability, because it's so hard and costly." What they likely have, he says, "is something closer to theories of behavior that by themselves might be quite sophisticated."

Theories of behavior are models that help us determine how the world and the creatures in it work, says Berns. "It's like if you're trying to cross the street in Manhattan, you don't need to get into the driver's mind. You just need to estimate the speed of the car."

On the other hand, "if you are trying to play a game of chicken with another driver, you might want to try to get into their head mentally to figure out what they're going to do. That's the difference between theory of behavior and theory of mind. And theory of mind requires a lot of mental effort."

It is important, says Berns, to take a middle view. "I think self-awareness is not an either/or phenomenon. I think it exists along a continuum and certainly all animals have to have some level of self-awareness." As both a dog lover and a scientist, however, Berns urges us to turn the question around. To not just wonder if dogs can put themselves in our shoes, but to ask ourselves if we can better put ourselves in their shoes, er, paws. "Anytime I'm trying to design an experiment or train a dog to do something or interpret what we see, I always have to remind myself to try to put myself in the dog's position, to see the world through the dog's eyes, not just through human eyes." A deeper understanding of a dog's world should bring benefits to dogs as well as to us.

IS MY DOG MAD AT ME?

Pet owners sometimes assume their dogs think like a person. There's some truth to that idea—but also plenty of fiction

BY HAYLEE BERGELAND, CPDT-KA, CBCC-KA, RBT

IF YOU'VE LIVED WITH A DOG, you understand how similar we humans are to our four-legged friends. We both love the best spot on the couch, eating delicious treats, and we *adore* getting new toys. But we dog owners often make the mistake of assuming our dogs think like we do or that our dogs "should just know better." When we attribute their behavior to something a human may do, we may be engaging in anthropomorphism.

Anthropomorphism is seeing human attributes in a thing or animal. We are hardwired to try to understand others from our own point of view, which is understandable and can help us connect with animals. But it can lead us to anthropomorphize our dogs in ways that aren't good for our pets.

YOUR DOG ISN'T LOOKING FOR REVENGE

Is it really so bad to attribute human qualities to our beloved pets? Well, a lot of punishment-based training is rooted in anthropomorphism. This kind of training attempts to justify "correcting" dog behavior by making up a story to explain the "misbehavior" (and what we should do about it), while in reality the interpretation has little or nothing to do with the real reason behind the pet's behaviors or actions.

For instance, a dog who pees on your guest's shoes by the door isn't trying to elevate himself over your guest in the household pecking order. Because that's not how dogs think. He's likely relieving stress caused by unfamiliar objects (and people) in the house.

"One of the most common forms of anthropomorphizing is not only treating dogs like humans but also adding in 'explanatory fictions' for a dog's behavior," says Randi Rossman, CBCC-KA, ACDBC, behavior and business executive at Canine Behavior Science.

Some people invent a reason for why the dog is reacting, which typically reflects what the person may think in a similar situation, not truly reflecting how a dog would think, she says.

Sometimes this even leads to an owner thinking that their dog's behavior has a deliberate, human-like motive, like spite or revenge. "Some people have created very complex explanatory fiction story lines for their dog's behavior. Others just can't understand why the dog would do a certain behavior because they don't know enough about dogs. And so [they] run through why a human might do such a thing and can't understand it," says Rossman. In the worst cases, this leads some people to harm their dogs through punishment and creates trust issues.

> ***"Dogs have similar emotional systems in the brains as we do, and so emotions like fear, which is a base for so many behavior challenges, isn't so terribly different for us than for dogs."***
>
> —RANDI ROSSMAN

COMMON DOG BEHAVIORS OWNERS JUST DON'T UNDERSTAND

Humping and mounting Dog owners are often embarrassed when their dog humps or mounts. They often think it's a sexual behavior or even suggests a dog's sexual orientation or sexuality. But humping has lots of functions. A dog may hump because it's excited, wants to play, is stressed or is overstimulated. Like tail-wagging, humping is full of nuance.

Growling Snarls, a quick growl, or a low, long growl are all very important, and natural, forms of dog communication. A dog that growls is telling you how it's feeling, and you should listen. Growls serve as a warning, not as a power move. Many times a dog is growling because it's extremely fearful and wants a human to listen.

Accidents (potty) Rest assured, dogs don't pee or poop in your house or their kennel because of malicious intent. A dog that has accidents in your house is unlikely to be fully potty trained, and you should never punish them for it. Accidents may stem from a dog that needs to be let outside more, or it could be due to a medical issue like a urinary tract infection.

Marking in the house Marking (small amounts of urine released) is an important and natural dog behavior. Scent marking is a way for dogs to communicate to one another and gain information about their environment. Dogs will mark in the house to create a familiarity and relieve stress when their environment changes.

Avoiding eye contact Yikes! All those "guilty dog" pics on social media might make you chuckle—like the pictures of a dog surrounded by a destroyed toilet paper roll. But if the owner just punished the dog, or screamed some choice words, the dog will avert his eyes to exhibit appeasement and stress behaviors, not guilt.

Taking a spot in bed or on the couch Dogs like to have comfortable places to take a snooze. This doesn't mean they want to take over your home. A dog that jumps onto the couch or tries to sleep in your bed just wants to be comfy.

IT'S NOT ALL BAD

Researchers feel anthropomorphizing can be unscientific, but within a dog-owner relationship it can be needed. For example, when a dog is feeling fearful or shy, "humanizing" a dog and its feelings can be helpful, even sensible. "It's okay to anthropomorphize when it helps build empathy for the dog, and also where there are similarities between humans and canines," Rossman says. "For example, dogs have similar emotional systems in the brains as we do, and so emotions like fear, which is a base for so many behavior challenges, isn't so terribly different for us than for dogs."

With a little help from positive reinforcement training, and understanding canine communication signals, you can avoid a lot of misunderstandings.

In John Pilley's home garden, Chaser is ready to pounce on her pile of toys, which she learned to categorize by function and form. Chaser died in 2019 at 15 years old.

Learning Through Playtime

Chaser had a way with words. In an excerpt by her owner and trainer, the late John Pilley, the psychologist describes how play was critical to Chaser's learning

BY JOHN PILLEY

HASER! THIS IS BLUE."

On my knees, I roll the blue racquetball toward her on the living room floor with no other toys anywhere in sight. As Chaser takes the ball in her mouth I repeat "Blue," the name of the ball. She begins to chew on it as I crawl toward her. When I'm close enough to reach out and grab the ball, she runs away, then turns and looks at me, wagging her tail and grinning.

In Chaser's first two months with Sally and me, she's demonstrated that she loves racquetballs, which happen to be blue in color, because they are so light and bouncy and feel so good in her mouth. And if I'm chasing her to get a racquetball, it must be very valuable. That makes playing keep-away with it exciting, fun, and, I hope, memorable.

"Blue," I whisper as I again reach for the ball. She darts just out of range again. Turning to look at me and wagging her tail in delight, she drops the ball accidentally and chases it as its bounces across the room.

Each time she takes the ball in her mouth I repeat its name: "Blue. That's Blue, girl, Blue." The ball bounces where I can grab it, and I am determined to teach her the name of the ball as I roll it to her, repeating, "Blue. Blue. Chaser, that's Blue!"

There was no road map in the scientific literature for teaching words and their meanings to a dog or any other animal. I began trying to teach Chaser words on the assumption that unless the words had strong positive value in her mind, she would not be motivated to focus on them and remember them. I reasoned that the best way to give words positive value was to associate them with objects used in play. Play would give the objects value, and by extension play would give value to the names of the objects and the verbs and other words that directed play activities.

Play should have many learning benefits, I knew. As a college professor, I had seen how play frees the mind from tension and anxiety, thereby opening the door to creative thinking.

I wanted to start language-related play with Chaser as soon as possible. Research has shown that there is a critical early developmental period for children to acquire language when they are toddlers, and I speculated that dogs might have a similar developmental window as puppies.

In anticipation of getting a puppy, I went to the local thrift store and bought a shopping cart full of secondhand children's and pet's toys: balls, stuffed animals, rubber animals and dolls, leather chew toys, pull toys, Frisbees, and so on. I was going to use these toys to teach Chaser proper nouns, words that uniquely name something or someone. Because of their strictly limited meaning and one-to-one association with something or someone, proper nouns, such as Mama, Dada, and their own names, were the first words toddlers learned. So I would begin teaching Chaser words with proper nouns, too.

I gave each object a proper noun name—Elephant, Lion, Santa Claus, and so on—and wrote the name on it in permanent ink. The only exceptions to my naming of toys were blue racquetballs and green tennis balls. Any racquetball was "Blue," and any tennis ball was "Tennis."

In the first two months after we got Chaser, I played with her with all of these toys. But I introduced each toy by name—"Chaser! This is Blue!"—one at a time, with no other objects on the floor available for play. Chaser responded enthusiastically to each new addition to her flock of playthings. She treated the objects like surrogate sheep and eagerly chased, stalked, fetched, and gathered them. She quickly learned the obedience and herding commands in the course of this play. Almost immediately she also started to show flashes of getting the name of an object into her short-term memory. Those moments really excited me, especially as they began to come more frequently and the memories began to be more long-lasting, extending from one play session to another a few hours later, and soon a day or more later.

> **Play would give the objects value, and by extension play would give value to the names of the objects and the verbs and other words that directed play activities.**

I wasn't yet seriously concentrating on teaching Chaser the proper noun names of the toys. Teaching her obedience behaviors took precedence in order to keep her safe from traffic and reliably direct her movements during training. I also wanted to build up the play value of the toys in her mind. And in that respect I was observing how she most liked to play with the toys and which ones she favored in different circumstances. With that information I could heighten her interest in a toy, and thus in its name, when we began training intensively.

I began to do more intensive training on the names of objects. The procedure began with Chaser sitting in front of me in the living room. So that Chaser could learn without errors and build on a series of small successes, the only toy in sight was a little stuffed Santa Claus doll that we'd played with many times, and whose name—Santa Claus—I had said dozens of times over the previous two months.

Holding up the doll and pointing to it, I said, "Chaser! This is Santa Claus."

Saying "Pop-Pop hide Santa Claus," I lowered the doll to the floor in plain view. Chaser's gaze never left it, and I trusted that she was giving me her ear and a glance of her eye. I dropped the doll on the floor and said, "Chaser, find Santa Claus," as she darted forward to pick it up in her mouth. "Good dog!" I told her. She looked up at me triumphantly, tail wagging, ears pricked up, and eyes bright and wide, eager to find out what was next.

Stepping back a few feet I said, "To Pop-Pop, to Pop-Pop. Here," beckoning her to me with outstretched arms. She came to me and let me take the doll from her

Chaser with his two teachers, Alliston Reid, the Reeves Family Professor of Psychology at Wofford College, and John Pilley, in 2011.

mouth, as I again said, "Good dog!"

Tossing the doll to her in a high arc, I said, "Chaser! Catch Santa Claus. Catch Santa Claus." She reared up on her hind legs to catch the doll, and as her front feet hit the ground again her tail went up and wagged back and forth with excitement and pleasure. "Good dog, good girl!" I said, positively reinforcing her.

"To Pop-Pop. Here," I said. She brought me Santa Claus, and her tail wagged faster at hearing another enthusiastic "Good dog!"

Finally I tossed Santa Claus into the middle of the living room and put Chaser through the herding behaviors: "Chaser, come by. Come by Santa Claus. Whoa. Way to me, way to me. There, there. Drop. Drop behind Santa Claus. Chaser, crawl to Santa Claus. There. Chaser, one, two, three, take Santa Claus! Good dog!"

After this herding play with as many repetitions of the name Santa Claus and as much positive reinforcement as possible, we began all over. To keep the game interesting I progressively hid Santa Claus so that the doll was harder and harder to find. In each word training session, consisting of a brief trial at finding Santa Claus and a few minutes of play with it, I said the name twenty to forty times.

Chaser with a selection of frisbees that she categorized by function. She learned a proper noun name for each one.

Over the course of the day's training sessions, we went through this exercise with Santa Claus at least twenty times.

Over the next few days we continued to play this game with Santa Claus. We also played the game with other objects that were already familiar to Chaser. The excitement of finding the object, whether it was hidden in plain view or in the other room, put a grin on both our faces and got Chaser's tail wagging with pleasure. After a brief moment to celebrate that victory, I rewarded Chaser with play with the object for three to five minutes. Depending on the object, the play might involve a little tug-of-war, chasing her as she scampered away with it, throwing it for her to catch or fetch, and, most of all, herding games. All the while, I repeatedly said the name of the object in very simple statements that described what we were doing and positively reinforced her with praise and pets: "Chaser, catch __. Good dog! Chaser, shake __. Good dog! Chaser, fetch __. Good girl, Chaser!"

After a few trials with different objects, Chaser knew what to expect, and her behavior briefly made me fear she had lost interest in what I was doing. When I said, "Chaser, this is __," she lay down on the floor and tilted her head as if she were completely ignoring the object and what I did with it. She remained lying on the floor, seeming utterly complacent, even bored. But as soon as I said, "Chaser, find __," she sprang to her feet and raced to find the object.

As she did so, I repeated, "Chaser, find __, Chaser, find __," in a soft, encouraging tone until she found it. This I greeted with a triumphant "Good girl, Chaser!" followed by a round of play with the object.

All told, our language training and testing sessions amounted to four to five hours a day. Weather permitting, I gave Chaser two to three hours of other physical activity a day outside the house. Some of the outdoor time was devoted to vigorous play with her named toys. But it also included agility play, tracking and stalking, and hikes in the nearby mountains.

“Chaser loved running the course, and my directions for her to run it in different directions and patterns were another opportunity to teach her words.

In the backyard I set up an agility course with jumps, a tunnel, obstacles to crawl under, and stakes to weave in and out of. Chaser loved running the course, and my directions for her to run it in different directions and patterns were another opportunity to teach her words. Every run through the course ended with my sailing a Frisbee for her to catch triumphantly.

Some days we took the forty-minute drive to sixty acres of forest we own on the Tyger River, southwest of Spartanburg, S.C. Chaser loved jumping over logs and exploring under bushes as we hiked to a spot on the river with a wide bank of flat rock. This was perfect wading water for her to splash into while retrieving sticks and balls I tossed for her. Walking the land, she darted here and there to investigate animal scents, always on the move, until we climbed back into the car, where she curled up and snoozed until we got home, at which point she was ready for round two.

At five months old Chaser knew more than fifty words, including those for the basic obedience behaviors. More important than the number was that we were both having lots of fun and she was eager to herd more toys, and more names, into her growing flock. Outside of training sessions, she often initiated play with her named toys and loved engaging in activities with them that mimicked herding sheep. A sequence of chasing, catching, bringing back, and gathering together a group of toys was deeply involving and rewarding for her.

As Chaser approached six months of age, intensive practice was speeding up her word learning so that she needed fewer and fewer trials per word. I could see her response time—animal scientists call it latency—getting shorter and shorter between the moment when I said, "Chaser, find __" and the moment when, eyes shining and tail wagging triumphantly, she brought back the correct surrogate sheep. She seemed to be learning words so quickly that I decided to try an extreme test.

I brought out a new object, a fleece-covered brown and white stuffed pony, about nine inches high and about fourteen inches from nose to tail. On the pony I had written the name Puddin. With Chaser sitting in front of me, I pointed to the stuffed pony and said, "Chaser! This is Puddin."

Then I immediately took it into the bedroom and placed it on the floor among seven other objects. Four were familiar objects whose names Chaser already knew, and three were novel objects she had never seen. Including three completely unfamiliar objects in addition to Puddin made the test very stringent, because it dramatically increased the possibility of error.

I came back in front of Chaser and asked her to find two of the previously learned objects, which she did without a hitch. There were still six objects on the floor in the other room: two familiar ones whose names she'd learned previously through repeated trials; three completely novel objects; and one, Puddin, that she'd seen and heard the name of only once. I then said, "Chaser, find Puddin."

Chaser sprang to her feet and dashed into the next room. In another flash of fur she stood before me wagging her tail and grinning from ear to ear with Puddin in her mouth. I immediately tested her twice more, and four more times the next two days. Each time I put Puddin down among a different set of seven other toys. Each time Chaser was perfect.

There was no doubt about it. Chaser had learned Puddin the pony's name in a single trial. Identifying the new object correctly after hearing its name only once indicated that Chaser had achieved a form of referential understanding. Somehow she had grasped the idea that objects can have names. She had learned that my pointing to an object and saying "This is " meant I was going to announce the object's unique name. To use the terms of childhood language learning research, Chaser had learned two referential social cues for indicating word meaning. On top of associative learning she had now added at least the first stage of intuitive learning via symbols. This was supposed to be impossible for nonhuman animals.

Chaser's intuitively understanding that objects can have names was a defining moment for her as a learner. Chaser did not consciously realize what had happened, any more than eighteen- to twenty-four-month-old toddlers consciously realize that they are suddenly understanding words in a new and fuller way. But I knew that Chaser had crossed a threshold and entered a whole new world of learning.

Random testing showed that Chaser could learn as many as ten new words a day, about as many as a nine-year-old child learns. Unlike a nine-year-old child, however, Chaser needed very extensive rehearsal time to retain this many words. So we settled into a pattern of one to two new words a day, which she could lock into long-term memory with a few days' worth of rehearsal sessions off and on through the day. Brief pilot testing suggested she could have learned three to four proper nouns a day, but I was also focusing on teaching her other elements of language, including common nouns and learning by exclusion.

At the age of seven and a half months, Chaser knew more than two hundred words. That Chaser was now reading my mind through the words I spoke to her gave me goose bumps. Seeing Chaser's vocabulary increase day by day and week by week, the goal for learning proper nouns was now a thousand words. A thousand-word vocabulary would be enough to show that Chaser's long-term memory system was extensive and robust. It was also enough to demonstrate her understanding of words as more than object names and in more contexts than simply fetching objects. If the skeptics didn't find Chaser's knowledge of a thousand proper nouns in combination with multiple common nouns and verbs convincing, they weren't going to be more favorably impressed by two thousand or three thousand proper nouns.

> **"Identifying the new object correctly after hearing its name only once indicated that Chaser had achieved a form of referential understanding.**

In the meantime I wanted to show [Border collie breeder] Wayne West what a smart puppy we'd gotten from him, and I wanted to talk to him about giving Chaser a chance to herd sheep.

I put about twenty of Chaser's toys in the back of my pickup truck and drove out with her to Wayne's place late on a mild fall afternoon. It was Chaser's first return to the place of her birth. She was now almost her full adult size, about twenty inches high at the shoulder, but she hadn't filled out to her full weight and strength yet. She was still very much a puppy. I saw no sign that she recognized the surroundings or Wayne. But true to her social nature, she was

Chaser, here in Pilley's Spartanburg, S.C., living room, could identify more than 1,022 toys.

delighted to get his warm welcome.

Wayne's backyard of nicely mown grass was separated by chain-link fencing from his kennel and barn area and the beginning of his pastures. Five sheep were in a large pen, about one quarter the size of a football field, next to his kennel. But Chaser paid no attention to the sheep or the dogs in the kennel as I got the plastic tub of her toys out of the back of my pickup and dumped them onto the grass. The appearance of her toys meant fun, and she kept her eye on her surrogate sheep.

Wayne watched in grave silence while Chaser retrieved one object after another by name and I directed her in herding-like play with them. Turning to Wayne, I said, "That's just a fraction of her learning. Right now she knows about two hundred words, and I'm thinking she can get to a thousand or more."

Wayne cracked a smile and said, "Doc Pilley, you've got a lot of patience." He wasn't at all surprised that a Border collie could learn a couple hundred words, and he didn't consider it a stretch for a Border collie to keep several hundred items straight in his or her mind. Working Border collies might have to distinguish individuals among hundreds of sheep from different flocks, and mingle or separate the flocks on command. He told me, "With you as a teacher, she'll hit the thousand mark and beyond. I don't have one iota of doubt about that. You're a dog man for sure, Doc."

I put Chaser's toys back in the plastic tub and stowed the tub in the pickup. Wayne was waiting for Chaser and me at the gate to the sheep pen. Even as we approached the gate, Chaser showed no particular interest in the sheep, who were grazing in a loose cluster twenty or thirty feet from the gate. She'd enjoyed our play with the toys and she walked at my side, tail up and wagging slightly, ready for some more fun, whatever that might be.

CAN DOGS SEE COLOR?

Brilliant rainbows, maybe not. But a canine's view of the world is a lot more than 50 shades of gray

BY HAYLEE BERGELAND, CPDT-KA, CBCC-KA, RBT

NOT EVERYTHING IS BLACK and white, even if you're a dog. Despite a long-held myth that dogs see the world through a gray lens, researchers now know that although our canine companions don't see the vast rainbow of colors we humans do, dogs don't see the world as though it's a vintage movie.

Dogs can see some colors, just not as many as we can. But just because you are lucky enough to see the beautiful changing leaves each fall doesn't mean your sight is superior. Dogs have excellent vision and have even evolved to see clearly in the dark.

WHAT IS COLOR BLINDNESS IN DOGS?

In the human sense of the word, dogs are color-blind, but in a very specific way. You might have heard that sometimes a person may have issues distinguishing red colors from green ones or perceiving shades of blue. This is due to color blindness and is commonly caused by a genetic issue within the eye or, later in life, an injury or illness. However, the way dogs see isn't because of any deficiency in the eye itself.

Humans and dogs both have two types of color receptors: cones and rods. The cones handle vision during the day and color perception. Rods tackle what can be seen at night and the ability to see from side to side and all around (peripheral vision). Each cone detects the wavelengths of light. Humans have three cones and so can generally detect the whole spectrum of light. Dogs have just two cones.

WHAT COLORS DO DOGS SEE?

A dog's two color-detecting cones help them to perceive blue and yellow light but not red or green. So in a dog's world view, they likely see everything as muted shades of yellow, brown, gray and tinges of blues. "Dogs can indeed see colors—it just looks a little different than it does for us," says Alicen Tracey, a small animal veterinarian at Den Herder Veterinary Hospital in Waterloo, Iowa.

Those bright red dog toys you always pick out? Well, your dog doesn't really see that bright red color. To them, that appears as one big hunk of brown.

"Dogs' vision of color most closely resembles that of people who have red-green color vision deficiencies," Tracey says. "For those with red-green color deficiency it is difficult to distinguish between the colors red and green."

WHAT DOES THIS MEAN FOR YOUR DOG?

It's really fun to pick out brightly colored dog toys, beds and collars. But while they are pleasing to us, their color likely makes no difference to your dog. Your dog doesn't need toys in rainbow hues, and those intense shades will not impact his toy preference—but it does seem to impact yours! Marketers and graphic designers know that humans prefer toys and pet gear in bright colors like red and orange, but dogs don't perceive those colors at all.

Some smart dog trainers and dog sport enthusiasts have picked up on the color scheme dogs perceive. For instance, you may have noticed that dog-agility equipment tends to be blue and yellow. In your own backyard, selecting Frisbees and balls that are yellow or blue could help your dog find them faster in green grass and foliage.

Have you ever found your dog barking in the dark, at what appears to be nothing, giving you just the right amount of creeps? Well, don't just dismiss the bark. Although dogs won't notice the bright red eye color of what you are positive is something menacing, they can see quite well in the dark. Their eyes may have fewer color-detecting cones than humans' eyes, but dogs have more light-sensitive rods. This means they can see creatures moving in the deep of the night. Which might be a handier skill for them than being able to appreciate the color of that fun new toy you just bought.

The Kindness of Canines

As scientists uncover the extent of mental cognition in dogs, your pet's emotional intelligence may be profound

BY EMILY JOSHU

SEVERAL YEARS AGO, Stanley Coren fell seriously ill. During that time, he had two dogs keeping him company. As Coren, who holds a PhD in psychology from Stanford University and is a professor emeritus in the University of British Columbia department of psychology, lay confined to his bed, Wiz, a Cavalier King Charles spaniel, remained close by. A gentle dog, Wiz had amassed a small collection of plush toys, including a fluffy sheep and a moose with one antler torn off by Wiz's brother, a cairn terrier. "If [the other dog] came over to those, it was the only time in history where Wiz would stand up and he would growl," Coren says. As he awoke one day, however, he found that Wiz had hopped up on the bed and had, one by one, stacked the toys atop his owner's stomach. "I felt that was one of the most diplomatic and caring gestures that I have ever encountered," Coren says.

To many dog owners, this display is familiar. Dog owners know that on their darkest days, whether due to illness, a breakup or tragedy, one thing's for certain: Fido will be right by their side, laying his head in their lap or offering to share his favorite toy. Much like a best friend, dogs sense these intense emotions—pain, heartbreak and so on—and want to do everything they can to make their owners feel better. In recent years, researchers have learned that this is because Fido is not only kind, but empathic. "Empathy is the ability of a mind to match the mood of another mind," says Carl Safina, PhD, endowed professor for nature and humanity at Stony Brook University and founding president of the not-for-profit Safina Center. "If someone next to you is upset or is injured or is in a good mood, you pick that up, and your mood reflects that."

Empathy is not an independent phenomenon. It exists on a spectrum with sympathy and compassion. While empathy is the process of feeling what someone else is feeling, sympathy is the act of feeling something for or on behalf of another person. Compassion, which is the most proactive level of the spectrum, is actively trying to help someone.

Empathy at any level has been traditionally considered a phenomenon exclusive to humans. But modern research has uncovered that a dog's capacity for empathic behavior may be why they can be so responsive to human emotions. Much of the research done on dogs' empathic capacity rests on what scientists know about the same sensations in toddlers. "The average dog has a mind equivalent to a human 2- to 2½-year-old," Coren says. "The superdogs, the top 20% of canine intelligence, have a mind equivalent to a 2½- to 3-year-old. So the question you have to ask yourself is, will a human 2- to 3-year-old show empathy?" True empathy, however, which is rooted in truly feeling what another is feeling, does not begin forming until a human child reaches the age of 4. "We would expect that a dog would have some signs of empathy just like a toddler would but not be able to necessarily express it completely," Coren says.

Additionally, the science behind dogs and empathy often involves utilizing the emotions of those most important to dogs: their owners. One 2017 study published in the journal *Animal Cognition*, for example, examined how dogs behaved differently after hearing nonemotional sounds of their environment versus emotional sounds from humans and other dogs. The results indicated that the dogs' responses to emotional sounds can be attributed to emotional contagion, meaning that the dogs were unconsciously able to mimic the emotions and expressions around them.

A landmark 2018 study in the journal *Learning & Behavior* called "Timmy's in the Well: Empathy and Prosocial Helping in Dogs" tested how dogs react to different emotions portrayed by their humans. The experiment involved 34 household dogs of various breeds. Owners stayed behind a clear door so that the dogs could see and hear them, and the owners were asked to either hum or cry. The researchers found that the dogs who opened the door when their owner was crying opened it three times faster than the dogs whose owners were humming. Additionally, the dogs who pushed through the door to "rescue" their owners had lower stress levels, meaning that while they were upset by the crying, they were not too upset to save their owner. "Every dog owner has a story about coming home from a long day, sitting down for a cry and the dog's right there, licking their face. In a way, this is the science behind that," said lead researcher Emily Sanford, a graduate student in the department of psychological and brain sciences at Johns Hopkins University.

Additional research has examined the brain activity in dogs by administering MRIs in an effort to compare the findings with those of humans. In some of these experiments, researchers have shown humans and dogs photographs of people whom they do or do not know. Safina, however, is doubtful of this method. "It's a little surprising to me that this seems to work with dogs, because dogs don't seem to me to be very visual, but I think they tend to just not show much of a reaction to visual things that they recognize," Safina says. "My guess is because those images don't smell like anything real, and they quickly discount them."

> **"The need for dogs to experience empathy is rooted in their ancestors. A wolf pack isn't all that different from a human family.**

WHAT ADVANTAGE DOES EMPATHY have for dogs? When it comes to everyday life, it is a necessity for animals who live in packs. "Essentially all animals that live in groups have to have empathy to coordinate what they're doing. So that if one startles or one alarms, the emotion spreads throughout the group," Safina says. "A group with no empathy is not a group; it's a bunch of individuals who are going to wander off in different directions."

Pack animals such as wolves and wild dogs will all react together, Safina says—a reaction that is caused by contagious fear. Contagious fear is, essentially, exactly what it sounds like. When someone feels fear, anxiety or stress, those around them pick up on that emotion and express it as well. If a dog or wolf becomes scared and flees, others in the pack will follow suit, having become susceptible to the "contagion" of fear. "That's what empathy is, so that if you feel someone next to you is upset or is injured or is in a good mood, you pick that up, and your mood reflects that. If they're startled, it startles you. You don't just stand there passively in the face of somebody being startled," Safina says.

This type of empathy can be seen in human behavior such as is reflected in the stock market and other mass activities. A 2020 study published in the journal *Frontiers in Psychology* examined

Contagious fear is what Carl Safina considers the oldest form of animal empathy. When a member of the pack picks up on a threat, the others can read that emotion and react.

the relationship between emotional contagion and anxiety around the COVID-19 pandemic. Among 603 college students, "individuals with greater levels of susceptibility to emotion contagion had greater levels of anxiety about COVID-19, more depression, anxiety and stress and greater levels of OCD symptoms," the researchers wrote.

The need for dogs to experience empathy is rooted in their ancestors. In his book *Beyond Words: What Animals Think and Feel,* Safina relates how he spent time observing the habits and family dynamics of wolves in Yellowstone National Park. In many respects, he says, a wolf pack isn't all that different from the average human family. "A wolf pack is just a nuclear family. It's mom and dad and their young ones from about the last two or three years," Safina says. "They're really very devoted to each other within the family." In his observations, Safina noticed intricate family and personality dynamics, as well as drama and tragedy. When two out of three adults in one wolf family were shot, the cohesion keeping the group together began to fall apart. Siblings began fighting and rejecting each other. The nuclear binding holding everyone together dissolved. "A lot of things that are subtle to us but should be familiar to us started happening to them, and I thought that was extremely eye-opening," Safina says.

These intricate ties are also present in our average household dogs. Even outside of a traditional pack, dogs are naturally inclined to protect and feel for each other. "You have to remember that dogs are social animals. We tend to think of empathy in terms of how our dogs

Researchers often compare the empathetic capacity of dogs to that of human toddlers. This emotional intelligence varies from one breed of dog to another.

respond to us, but they also tend to show empathy toward other dogs," Coren says.

THE EMPATHETIC NATURE OF DOGS could explain why they can be so comforting when we need them most, such as in times of sadness. Coren points to the idea of positive regard, coined by 20th-century psychologist Carl Rogers as a means of understanding why Fido really is man's best friend. When someone displays positive regard, they act in a supportive manner and consider those around them to have value. This can be broken into two categories, known as contingent positive regard and unconditional positive regard. Contingent positive regard involves praising someone based on good things that they have done, whereas unconditional positive regard is showing an individual affection and support even if they have done nothing to earn it. "Rogers always said that the most important kind of regard from a therapeutic sense, in order to make your life happier, is unconditional positive regard, where that regard comes no matter what's happening. And that's what we've bred our dogs to do," Coren says.

Many researchers claim that anthropomorphism, or the attribution of human thoughts and emotions to nonhumans, plays a role in how and why empathy is studied in dogs. Subtle ways of anthropomorphizing pets include things that humans do for their pets that they believe will benefit them. For modern dog owners, this includes putting clothes on dogs or leaving the television on when dogs are left alone in the house. In the 1890s, British researcher Conwy Lloyd Morgan believed it was wrong to explain animal behavior with "a higher psychical faculty" than demanded by the data. In the United States, Edward Thorndike argued that, when studied in controlled and replicable environments, animal behavior revealed simple mechanical laws that would deem more mentalistic explanations unnecessary, according to a 2004 article in *Nature* by Clive D.L. Wynne. Some psychologists discourage anthropomorphizing animals and focus solely on cognitive approaches and observation.

More recently, the perspective on anthropomorphism has shifted. A 2007 article by experts Alexandra C. Horowitz and Marc Bekoff argues that we, as humans, have been shaped by natural selection to view animal behavior through an anthropomorphic lens. To Safina, treating anthropomorphism as taboo is too great a limitation. "That to me is not science," he says. "Science is not supposed to have rules about what you're allowed to believe. Science is supposed to believe what the evidence shows. If animals actually do have thoughts and if they have emotions, and they are some of the same emotions that humans have, like fear or a sense of well-being or happiness or fun or rage, then you're not projecting them; you're observing that they have those emotions."

Coren relates the debate surrounding anthropomorphizing to the manner in which researchers study dogs: by looking at human toddlers. Observing and interpreting the behaviors of human toddlers, Coren argues, is hardly dissimilar from how anthropomorphism is applied to dogs. "If we completely removed anthropomorphism, we would lose our ability to fully study the animals, especially dogs," he says.

Like humans, not all dogs have the same capacity for empathy. This can be attributed to individual personalities and, more widely, to differences among breeds. "Certain breeds of dogs, particularly those which we tend to think of as companion dogs, have been specifically bred by us … to be empathic," Coren says. Toy dogs, such as Pomeranians, have been bred to be more empathetic, as well as sporting breeds, such as retrievers and spaniels.

> **"We would expect that a dog would have some signs of empathy just like a toddler would."**
>
> —DR. STANLEY COREN

These breeds also tend to be ideal therapy animals "because the essence of a therapy dog is to be highly sociable and responsive to the individual's needs," Coren says. "If dogs didn't have empathy, they would be absolutely useless as therapy dogs." The key to an ideal therapy animal, Coren says, is its ability to be sociable and attentive, so as to effectively respond to how a person communicates and what emotions the person is feeling. A therapy dog's level of empathy may also help it to tolerate certain human behaviors. For instance, if a patient with a motor disability accidentally tugs on the dog's ear, the dog will still stay by the patient's side to support them. "The dogs who turn out to be the best therapy dogs are the ones who are most forgiving," Coren says.

This level of empathy might also explain why dogs are the standard for therapy animals, and not cats or other domesticated mammals—let alone turtles, snakes, parakeets or other common pets. These animals are generally more aloof and less social, Coren says, so they do not have the same capacity for empathy that Fido has.

SO HOW DO YOU KNOW IF YOUR DOG is showing you empathy? Chances are, the signs are in the ways in which they shower you with affection every day. If your dog is acting clingy, following you around the house, inviting you to play or cuddling up to you on the couch, they are showing that they know they have a relationship with you. "They know that you have intentions. They show you intentions. You can easily see what it is that they want and what it is that they need and what it is that they are asking you for," Safina says.

Sometimes the most caring gesture your furry friend can give is just checking to see if you're okay. Recently, while working in the yard, Safina slipped and fell down. His dog immediately rushed over to him, sniffing him and licking him. "It was very obvious that she knew that something had gone wrong," Safina says. "That I might be hurt, was what I think she was concerned about. If you think about what the human response to somebody falling is and then you subtract the words, the dog's response was identical."

WHO'S SMARTER: CATS OR DOGS?

While scientific researchers wrestle with studies defining animal intelligence and comparing species, these two veterinarians have a little fun with their take on what's really special about your favorite pooch's particular brand of smarts

BY BRENDAN HOWARD

YOU LOVE YOUR DOG. SO YOU want your dog to be smart—smarter than cats, more clever than your least favorite relatives, and certainly picky enough to pick you as his No. 1 favorite human. But if you want proof dogs are smarter than cats and to know if your dog is particularly brainy, our veterinary experts have some serious (and perhaps disappointing) opinions on this.

ARE CATS SMARTER THAN DOGS?

To find out, one researcher

When it comes to loyalty and the "smarts" behind social connection and bonding, maybe dogs win.

counted neurons in brain tissue: cats had less, dogs had more. The more neurons, the more capacity for thinking, tasks and intelligence, right? Sure, but to do what? Animals are smart enough to survive in the world they live in. If one animal can use tools, another animal picks up on your emotions, and a third picks up on your hand motions—well, which is smarter?

Another researcher checked to see if pets would look at something you pointed at and figure out you wanted them to look at it; dogs, for sure, did, but—surprise!—cats did, too.

It turns out that veterinarians who've spent years looking at domestic cats have opinions about how smart and special your feline friends are. Remember, these veterinarians are a little biased (like you), because they love all the ways that cats show preference, cleverness and connection with people.

WHAT MAKES CATS SMART?

Anna Foster, doctor of veterinary medicine with the national hospital chain Veterinary Emergency Group, says it comes down to what you value. When it comes to loyalty and the "smarts" behind social connection and bonding, maybe dogs win. (Stories about senior dogs hovering around their owner's graveside are not uncommon and sure to make you cry.) But if we're talking about hunting in the wild, cats win. (Does your cat need you around to go hunting when he wants to snatch bugs, lizards, birds and other small animals? Nope.)

Cats don't need you to have a good time, according to Foster. "The ability to think and act independently? Cats have this. They wait for you to walk away before they do stuff." Kelly St. Denis, current president of the American Association of Feline Practitioners, thinks a cat's independence make him ruler of the roost: "Dogs have masters. Cats have staff."

"This obviously suggests that cats are smarter, because they employ—rather than serve—humans," St. Denis jokes.

This board-certified feline veterinarian says cats can learn tricks (like dogs), may know more human words than we thought and develop special meows, trills and chirps to communicate with their staff (er, owners).

Dogs seem to win out in these discussions because they learn what we want and do it. Cats are different.

"Cats have a specific agenda and seem to require that we mold ourselves to their plans, not the other way around," St. Denis says.

The alluring aloofness and independence cats display doesn't mean they need less medical care than more vocal, more attentive pooches. Cats' independence can mask disease and illness, says St. Denis.

"Humans often assume that because cats are not complaining and are so independent, that they don't need to see a veterinarian," she says. "Their ability to hide illness makes their visits to the vet all the more critical."

WHICH CAT BREEDS ARE THE SMARTEST?

If you're a smart cat owner in need of a particularly talented feline, there are a few smart cat breeds with particular dispositions that might make a fabulous fit for you. Some cats, like Siamese, are big talkers. Other breeds, like Abyssinian, Scottish fold and Savannah cats, are addicted to play. And Tonkinese love attention. This doesn't mean every member of these breeds match these exact characteristics, but you may have a better shot at a better fit.

The Power of Thinking Like My Dog

Move over, Tony Robbins. I have a new motivational guru, and he barks

BY DAN BOVA

EMILY DICKINSON wrote that hope is the thing with feathers. If that's true, then my shredded down winter jacket on the basement floor is completely hopeless. But the perpetrator of the criminal act that left my formerly puffy coat deflated? He has hope in spades. He has hope stuck to his face, his fur, and presumably inside his stomach. I'm talking about my 7-month-old puppy, Clark. Clark is a Havanese, which is a Cuban breed that roughly translated means "eater of everything." There is not a substance of the periodic table of elements that Clark isn't interested in chewing. Remote controls? Yum. The cheeseburger in your hand? Oh baby. The shoes you were going to return but now can't because the box is ripped apart and covered in dog drool? Seconds please!

I'm not sure if Clark's desire to constantly eat things is nature or nurture (after all, he does live with two teenage human brothers who regularly attack our pantry's snack shelf with the wild desperation of half-starved hyenas). But I will say this: while his penchant for turning everything he sees into puppy chow is annoying and enraging, I have to admit that there is part of me that also finds it inspiring. This dog is absolutely open to possibilities of finding joy in every new thing he chomps. And beyond snacking, everything he does, sniffs and jumps on top of. He's willing to give it a shot no matter what previous results have been. And let me tell you, the results are not always favorable.

Never Look Back

A few months ago, Clark grabbed something out of the kitchen garbage can while we were all too exhausted to be monitoring him 24/7. We didn't know what it was, but we knew it was big. He looked like a squirrel with a year's worth of acorns crammed in his cheeks. As my son Gus and I begged, "Drop it! Drop it!" Clark smiled at us through clenched teeth and then swallowed like a character in a Looney Tunes cartoon. Gulp! A quick archaeological dig in the trash revealed that there was a very real possibility that a very large piece of chicken (including the bone) now resided in his tummy. "Don't all dogs eat bones?" I asked. "Is it really a big deal?" Yes, it is a big deal, answered a Google search.

Twenty minutes later, I was standing in front of a veterinarian at the doggy ER. She pointed to the X-ray of Clark's stomach, showing what appeared to be a pterodactyl wing jammed wall to wall in his little puppy tummy. "There is no way that is coming out the other end," she explained. Then she showed me the estimate of how much it would cost to surgically remove it. Without revealing the exact number, I will say that for the same price, I could have purchased a pretty nice pre-owned Hyundai.

Our puppy smiled at us through clenched teeth, then swallowed the bone like a character in a cartoon. Gulp.

I fell in love with my wife the day I met her. That love grew the day of our wedding and grew even more when she gave birth to our beautiful boys. But I don't think I've loved her quite as much as when she told me over the phone at 2 a.m. that the pet insurance she insisted on getting for Clark would cover 90% of the bill. "Cut it out, doc!"

After two weeks of living with a cone around his head and taking pain meds that turned him into an extra from *Breaking Bad*, Clark learned his lesson. And that lesson was this: garbage-can chicken is delicious and there must be more things like it. When we're out on walks, and he comes across a discarded surgical mask, the risk of it sending him to the ICU is far exceeded by the chance that the person wearing it used it as a napkin to wipe the remains of their tuna sandwich off their face before they tossed it in the street. He doesn't look back. Baggage from the past will never get in the way of his future happiness.

Living in the Moment

Nowhere is Clark's driven desire for something good to eat more on display than in the kitchen. I know that sounds obvious, but let me explain. Anytime, and I mean anytime, anyone in our household opens the refrigerator door, he comes racing in. He could be chasing dream chipmunks in the deepest puppy sleep in the basement, but when that refrigerator door seal pops, he is on his feet and in full sprint. Before you can decide if you are going to go with a healthy midday apple or a slice of shame salami, he is at your feet, staring up at you. He doesn't beg. He doesn't whine. He just watches and waits. Anything can happen.

Maybe as my son prepares some nachos, a few sprinkles of cheese will miss the tray and wind up in striking distance. Perhaps a butter stick will lose its perch and fall from the sky like a scene from *Cloudy with a Chance of Meatballs*. Who knows?

These happy accidents don't happen every day, but like the great Wayne Gretsky he seems to realize that you miss 100% of the shots you don't take. The perfect napping spot in the sunbeam and the fantasy chipmunks will still be there in five minutes, but it could be hours before that refrigerator door opens again.

No Labels

Clark's hope that joy awaits around every corner isn't limited to his unlimited appetite. He is unusually open to new experiences and quite willing to take the advice of those motivational speakers who implore us all to get out of our comfort zones. Clark, as I have mentioned, is a dog. But on some days, he likes to try out different animal behaviors that he's perhaps not suited for. This dog likes to climb on things (or try to climb on things) as if he were a cat. Ever see a cat gracefully dance across the back of a couch with the effortless grace of a master thief in *Ocean's Eleven*? Clark tries that all the time, and as evidenced by the thuds you routinely hear echoing through the house, he's not so much with the gracefulness. But no matter how many times gravity and his lack of coordination get the best of him, he climbs back up on the back of that couch because . . . I don't know. I honestly don't know what he hopes to achieve. Is it a Sir Edmund Hillary explaining he wanted to climb Everest "because it's there" kind of thing? Possibly.

Welcoming New Friendships

Out on walks, Clark greets every dog he passes as a potential new best friend. He gets very, very, very excited when he spots a fellow four-legger and will stalk and drag us for blocks if necessary to catch up. Clark really puts himself out there. There are no half-hearted, cool-guy head nods to protect his ego from rejection. He gives the doggy equivalent of a giant hug and a "Pleased to meet you!" to every mammal he meets. This comes in the form of sticking his face directly into his new acquaintance's junk and inhaling deeply. Sometimes the dogs happily sniff back; others aren't so keen to have a complete stranger poking around down there. They snap at him, they bark—and he's fine with that! No wounded pride. No hurt. He just moves on to find his next potential buddy. Whether it is a tiny toy poodle or a giant Great Dane that could inhale him with one nostril, he is utterly fearless—the embodiment of the love-seeking strategy that says if you ask 100 people out, and 99 say no, congrats, you have a date!

Never Let Anyone Take Anything Away From You

Speaking of romance, Clark recently went to the vet to receive some elective surgery. Not the kind that results in a perky new nose—the kind that Bob Barker pleaded for at the close of nearly every episode of *The Price Is Right*: "Have your pets spayed or neutered." Nothing pleasant has ever happened to Clark at the veterinarian. He's gotten shots, had his anal glands expressed (you don't want any details on that, I assure you) and experienced all kinds of other not-so-fun poking and prodding. Yet whenever they open the door at the vet's office, he runs in, tail wagging and tongue doing twirls. He doesn't know what is about to happen—every single time it's been awful—but maybe this time it will be awesome!

I felt bad for him as he happily marched in for the Big Snip. Yes, we hoped it would help mute some of his higher-energy quirks, but I was mildly worried that his post-surgery existence would be akin to Austin Powers having his mojo stolen by Dr. Evil. Would he turn into a listless blob who was more "meh" than "Yeah, baby!"?

My fears subsided soon enough. When the post-surgery painkillers wore off, Clark's first newly neutered act was to wobble over to his favorite furry dog bed, and then, as if the lights dimmed and a Barry White track faded up from the quiet, he began furiously humping it. If that doesn't say hope, I don't know what does. 🐾

EXCERPTED FROM *REAL SIMPLE THE POWER OF POSITIVITY: A SIMPLE OUTLOOK CAN CHANGE YOUR LIFE*, AVAILABLE ON MAGAZINE.STORE AND AMAZON.

Chapter Two

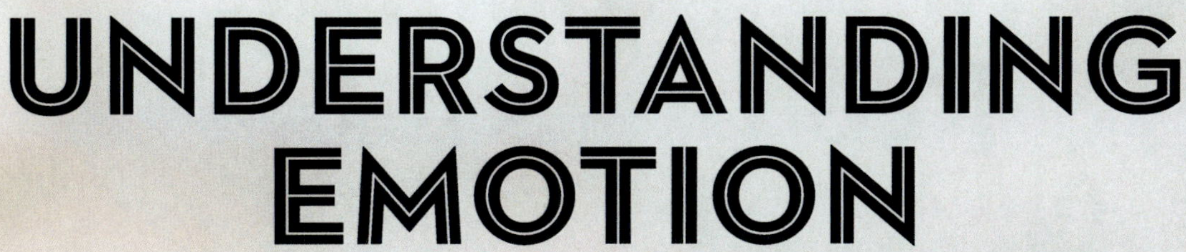

UNDERSTANDING EMOTION

Dogs can experience joy and comfort, but also suffer from mental health disorders. Insight into their emotional capacities sheds light on the impact of human actions

How's Your Dog *Really* Feeling?

Just because your dog can't say "I'm sad" or "I'm anxious," doesn't mean he's not experiencing emotional turmoil. Here's how to help your furry friend out

BY HOLLY PEVZNER

WE ALL KNOW DOGS can do wonders for our mental health. Service dogs can help alleviate symptoms of post-traumatic stress disorder. Therapy pups have been shown to reduce stress in students, health-care workers and others. Even your average house dog can considerably quell anxiety and sadness, all while improving happiness, according to a 2019 study in the journal *Animals*. And a more recent report found that 70% of folks credit their dog for helping them cope with loneliness and depression brought on by the pandemic. So, yeah, dogs are the best. But they're not immune to their own mental-health woes.

"Just like humans, dogs can most certainly suffer from mental-health conditions, such as anxiety and depression," says Stephanie Borns-Weil, DVM, DACVB, a veterinary behaviorist and clinical assistant professor at Tufts University Cummings School of Veterinary Medicine in North Grafton, Mass. "But unlike humans, dogs can't describe to us what they're feeling and thinking." Instead, they do things like incessantly chase their tails, lunge at the neighbor, refuse walks or cower under the sofa. And while we often see these types of habits as silly little quirks or behavior problems, the reality is that "most of these actions are rooted in some underlying psychological issue," says veterinary behaviorist Nicholas Dodman, BVMS, DACVB, president of the Center for Canine Behavior Studies in Salisbury, Conn. The good news? The signs are there and help is in reach. We just need to know what we're looking for.

When Depression Strikes

"Sadly, depression in dogs is more common than most people think," says Borns-Weil. Much like their owners, dogs can become blue following a variety of life changes, such as the loss of a loved one or a fur buddy, a move, or any kind of a disruption in routine. Things like chronic stress and anxiety and a lack of predictability can spur depression, too. So can complete and utter boredom, which can be especially true for high-energy, driven breeds who thrive on physical or mental stimulation, such as herding dogs, boxers, Golden Retrievers, Dobermans and Great Danes, notes the American Kennel Club (AKC). "With Covid lockdowns, many of us learned first-hand how much our mental health suffered from not going to work, attending exercise classes, going to services, meeting with friends and doing other human things," says Borns-Weil. "It's the same for dogs. A lack of opportunities to do doggie things can easily cause or contribute to depression."

You don't have to be an expert to spot signs of depression in your dog. You simply need to tune into what's normal for your pups, so you can see when abnormal behavior arises. Has your terrier's appetite waned? Is your doodle-mix less interested in fetch or heading to the park? Is your pug sleepier than usual? Has your chocolate lab started following you around the house? All of these may be signs of depression. "If you see these or really any behavior changes in your dog, visit the vet," says Borns-Weil, noting that pain and discomfort are very common causes of depression, making a vet visit imperative.

If there is a physical explanation for your pup's mood, proper treatment steps will be taken. "And if pain is a possibility, but no clear cause is apparent upon a physical exam or testing, your vet may still

Many dogs chase their tails, but for some the behavior is a sign of the canine version of OCD. If your dog circles for hours on end or seems obsessive, get in touch with your vet.

suggest a trial course of analgesics, or painkillers," says Daniel S. Mills, PhD, professor of veterinary behavioral medicine at the University of Lincoln, in the U.K. "Of course, you have to assess the clinical picture first, but I'd say that about 80% of the behavior issues I see in my own practice, including depression, are in some way related to pain." No illness or injury? Then your vet may suggest you make some changes at home.

"If the problem is due to something like lack of social engagement or insufficient stimulation or exercise, then fixing those problems will help the dog get his or her groove back," says Borns-Weil. For instance, a report in the journal *PLOS One* notes that exercise increases production of the feel-good hormone serotonin in animals, thus functioning as a doggie antidepressant. That said, "there are many dogs who live with people who really do provide optimal care for their dogs who are still depressed," says Borns-Weil. "Dogs, like people, can exhibit depressive behavior for a variety of reasons, like genetics or early life trauma where, say, the dog was mistreated, didn't get their needs met as a young puppy, or trained by people who used pain, threat or fear." For those pups, treating underlying anxiety or post-traumatic stress with vet-led behavior modification and, in some cases, psychoactive medication, may be best, says Borns-Weil.

When Tail-Chasing Becomes Extreme

German shepherds and terriers are prone to chasing their tails and spinning. Herding breeds, like Border collies, are more apt to go after light and shadows. Meanwhile, "Dobermans tend to grab on to their upper thigh with their mouth, called flank sucking. And several other large breed dogs tend to focus on licking their limbs," says

Dodman. All of these dog activities are totally normal. That is, "if they're done in moderation or for a specific purpose," says Amanda Williams, DVM, chief veterinarian and medical director at Furry Friends Adoption, Clinic & Ranch in Jupiter, Fla. But when these behaviors become excessive and difficult to stop, then your dog may have canine compulsive disorder (CCD), the dog version of obsessive compulsive disorder (OCD). Other signs of CCD include pacing, freezing and staring, endlessly sucking on a toy or drinking water, snapping at invisible items, nonstop barking and various forms of self-mutilation. "This is when a dog licks or bites themselves to an extreme, causing injury," says Williams. "Like if your dog licks the same spot repeatedly, causing skin issues and bald patches, or chases and bites his tail to the point that it's damaged and may need to be amputated." Self-mutilation is actually the most common CCD behavior in dogs, according to a 2020 study in the journal *Scientific Reports*.

The same report found that overall 16% of dogs exhibit CCD behaviors, with German shepherds, mixed-breed dogs and Staffordshire bull terriers impacted the most. "To some extent, the compulsive behaviors in these dogs are based on genetics and on the function for which the breed was developed," says Dodman. For instance, the AKC notes that when working dogs—like the light-chasing collie—find themselves job-free, compulsive behaviors might surface. Furthermore, it seems that dogs with CCD (like humans with OCD) may have a hiccup in their serotonin transmission, which impacts the ability of brain and nervous system cells to communicate with each other. Plus, research in the journal *Progress in Neuro-Psychopharmacology & Biological Psychiatry* found that the flank-sucking Doberman pinschers with CCD display similar underlying structural brain abnormalities as people who have OCD.

Similarly to doggie depression, compulsive behaviors in dogs can sometimes be due to an underlying medical condition. In fact, self-mutilation is often spurred by allergies, fleas or another skin issue. Other times, CCD is an extreme reaction to a lack of physical or mental stimulation, high anxiety or frustration. No matter what might be the cause, CCD can be difficult to diagnose. Not only can dogs not tell us what they're obsessing about, but "many dog owners simply don't know what's normal and what's abnormal, so it's difficult to recognize when they're behaving in an obsessive manner," says Borns-Weil. If you suspect CCD may be in play, try to catch your dog's obsessive behavior on video to help the vet diagnose the issue. (Also, keep a record of when and how often the behaviors occur, and whether a specific situation seems to domino the reaction.)

"Oftentimes, environmental treatment of OCD-like behaviors can be helpful," says Dodman. "That means providing the dog an enriched environment that caters to their biological needs. For example, a light-chasing Border collie may stop the behavior entirely if regularly taken to sheep-herding classes." For others, increasing daily exercise can be very helpful. "If these types of treatments don't work, medication is another possible route," says Dodman. "In that context, human anti-obsessional drugs like Prozac or drugs that limit the activity of the neurotransmitter glutamate, like Namenda, are helpful."

Could It Be Anxiety?

"Anxiety in dogs is just as common as anxiety in people," says Ragen T.S. McGowan, PhD, pet behavior research scientist for Purina in St. Joseph, Mo., who notes that all dogs can experience anxiety from time to time. In fact, anxiety-related problems occur in 44% of dogs, according to a 2019 report in the journal *Canine Research*, and a 2018 Purina survey eked that number up, with 62% of dog owners saying that their dog demonstrated at least one anxious behavior. (Separation anxiety, PTSD, fear of new situations, thunderstorm or loud-noise stress, and more all fall into the anxiety bucket.)

According to Dodman, herding dogs tend to show more fearful or anxious behaviors than other breeds, but doggie anxiety can affect all pups. And despite what you may have heard, small dogs are not more anxious than their larger counterparts. "It's just that they're in public more often than big dogs, so their anxious behavior is more visible," says McGowan. Like humans, dogs have different personalities and temperaments that influence the way they react to things that go on in their day-to-day life. "But one of the most powerful instigators of anxiety is experiencing an adverse event or circumstances during the sensitive period of learning, which is arguably the first six months of life," says Dodman. (Spending long hours alone in a crate or being re-homed multiple times are examples of early adversity.) As such, some puppies will display anxious temperaments early on, "while others develop anxious behavior later due to new or disruptive changes to their environment or routine," says McGowan. For instance, as much as our dogs loved the extra attention they received when so many of us were working from home during the pandemic, it very much disrupted their routine. "This exacerbated existing anxiety in some dogs and caused it in others," says McGowan, whose own dogs took their role as family protectors a bit too seriously during quarantine, becoming overly anxious and barking at the window when the slightest thing happened outside.

Excessive barking is far from the sole symptom of anxiety. "You may notice your dog's ears pressed flat against their head or worried facial expressions that could be an averted gaze; pupils widely dilated; or whale eye, when the whites of the dog's eyes appear in a half-moon shape at the inner or outer side of the eye," says Dodman. Other clues include drooling, panting, potty accidents, restlessness, destructive behavior and aggression. The previously mentioned study in *Scientific Reports* found that anxious and fearful dogs were 3.2 times more aggressive than nonfearful dogs. And, according to Dodman, "aggression is often a result of unpleasant earlier experiences, including PTSD."

"The very best way to treat your dog's anxiety is to visit the veterinarian," says Dodman, who advises recording a video of your dog's behavior for your vet. They'll be able to help you zero in on the type of anxiety your pupper is dealing with and, hopefully, uncover causes and triggers in order to land on the perfect treatment option. After all, recovery plans for, say, the 19% of dogs that have anxiety because of crowds will not be the same as for the 31% of dogs who are dealing with anxiety related to noise and thunderstorms. And while sometimes-anxious pups may not require intervention, know that "animals who are in a chronic vigilant state have higher levels of circulating hormones such as cortisol," says McGowan. These kinds of chronic, unchecked and excessive levels of anxiety can spur a full-blown anxiety disorder in your pup, according to the AKC. And research in the journal *Applied Animal Behaviour Science* has shown that anxiety disorders can have detrimental effects on the health and lifespan of your dog.

What Looks Like Separation Anxiety May Be Something Else

About 17% of dogs experience separation anxiety, notes a 2019 report in the *Journal of Veterinary Behavior*. With separation anxiety, it appears as though your dog is wound up about being left alone, as manifested in such unpleasant behaviors as potty accidents, destruction and endless barking. But sometimes what looks like separation anxiety really isn't. A 2020 report in the journal *Frontiers in Veterinary Science* notes that various forms of frustration, like boredom, wanting to get to something out of reach or reacting to outside noises, are likely the heart of the issue. "Try setting up a doggie cam to see if this can help you discern the cause," says McGowan. And next time you leave your pup home, "provide him with a lot of things to occupy his time, like treat-stuffed toys, cognitive puzzles or dog toys designed to pull apart, which can help with boredom," says McGowan. These fun things also act as what's dubbed counterconditioning, which means you're helping your dog develop a positive association with your leaving. Each time you head for work, pups get a yummy treat or a fun puzzle to play with.

What to Do About Noise Anxiety

While noise sensitivity is most common in Lagotto Romagnolos (a.k.a. Italian water dogs), wheaten terriers and mixed breeds, a bright boom of fireworks or a loud clap of thunder causes problems for about one third of all dogs, according to research. Big noises can be rough on a dog's acute sense of hearing and the unpredictability of certain noises keeps dogs on edge, triggering their fight-or-flight response, notes McGowan. Luckily, noise phobia can often be treated using desensitization and counterconditioning. "This means increasing exposure to the feared sound in an incremental way under pleasant circumstances. And pairing exposure to the feared sound with delicious treats to create a positive association," says Dodman. (For example, play low-level fireworks sounds while playing with your pups and offering treats.) Another approach: provide your dog a safe place shielded from the noise. "Think tornado bunker, fully equipped with the things your dog loves, including you, food, toys and white noise," says Dodman. In addition, thundershirts can be an effective tool to help someone cope with stressful situations. "Just as swaddling works to soothe infants, the constant low pressure of a thundershirt can be very soothing to nervous dogs," says McGowan. Perhaps most important, a 2018 report in the journal *Frontiers in Veterinary Science* stressed that dogs

Vets can't prescribe CBD products, but they may be able to recommend CBD products if needed for your dog. Follow your vet's advice.

who show fear or anxiety when faced with loud or sudden noises should be assessed for pain by their veterinarians. It's thought that dogs with certain types of chronic pain may tense their bodies when startled by noise, exacerbating discomfort.

Will CBD Help?

According to a 2019 report out of Colorado State University in Fort Collins, anxiety and noise aversion are two of the most common reasons pet owners seek cannabidiol (CBD), which is a compound found in cannabis and hemp, for their dogs. Right now, however, the question of whether CBD can aid canine mental health remains unanswered. "Scientific studies on this matter are still in their infancy," says Williams. "That said, anecdotally, those who've administered CBD to their dogs have reported that it has helped with issues like seizures, nausea and anxiety." If you are interested in trying CBD with your dog, talk it over with your vet first. "Look for an oil or a tincture that has little to no THC and that's free from pesticides, fungicides, solvents and additives," says Williams. "And high-quality CBD products are often expensive, but you don't want to jeopardize your dog's health to save a couple of bucks," says Williams. (Always introduce it in small doses to see if your dog has an adverse reaction.)

In the end, "know that if your dog is misbehaving in some way or acting out of the ordinary, that doesn't always mean that your pet is willful or stubborn or dominant—or that it's your fault," says Borns-Weil. "It may simply mean that your dog needs a diagnosis—and your help." After all, while a dog is for sure man's (and woman's) best friend, we're their best buds, too. We owe it to them to take their mental health as seriously as our own.

Does My Dog Have Anxiety?

Are your dog's "misbehaviors" signs of anxiousness? Here's what to know and when to get help

BY HAYLEE BERGELAND, CPDT-KA, CBCC-KA, RBT

YOU MAY BE ATTUNED to signs of your own anxiety; you feel nervous, quick to anger, overly tired or just on edge. Canines experience anxiety much in the same way we do, and being a dog parent with an anxious pup isn't fun for anyone.

For some dogs, feeling anxious is a passing experience—maybe it only occurs on Thanksgiving. (Your relatives and their chaos bother your dog, too.) But if your dog can't be left home alone without issues or appears distressed at any changes in their schedule, they could have a severe, diagnosable form of anxiety—and will need a good treatment plan to feel better.

Here's what pet parents should know about anxiety and how to recognize when it's time to seek additional help.

What Is Anxiety?

"From a clinical perspective, there are two primary patterns of anxiety," says Christopher Pachel, DVM, DACVBM, CABC, a veterinary behaviorist at the Animal Behavior Clinic in Portland, Ore. Broadly speaking, the patterns break down into situational anxiety and generalized anxiety. "Situational anxiety occurs in specific situations or contexts. For instance, your dog may become anxious when she's left alone (separation anxiety) or when she is left at the boarding facility. Generalized anxiety doesn't depend on one particular context or event," Pachel says.

When a dog's anxiety becomes severe and hinders the pooch's quality of life, it's advisable to consult with a veterinary behaviorist or certified animal behavior consultant.

A quick note about fear: "Although fear and anxiety often get lumped together, they are actually completely separate emotional states," Pachel says. Fear is an emotional state, something that an animal or human feels after a trigger or during an unpleasant event, like being spooked after a sudden lightning crash. Anxiety is a buildup of strong emotions and worrying about a potential threat or event, like hearing rain drops and then worrying a big storm is coming even if there's no sign of thunder or lightning.

What Does Anxiety in Dogs Look Like?

When a dog is really anxious, they may engage in behaviors that look like "misbehaving," but are actually signs of anxiety. It's important to never correct or punish a dog for being anxious.

While this isn't an exhaustive list of all the signs of more severe anxiety, here are some indicators that a dog is experiencing anxiety in some form.

- Hiding/fleeing/avoidance. Attempts to hide, escape or avoid stimuli.
- Freezing. Becoming stiff and immobile at the sight of stimuli.
- Heavy breathing or panting.
- Excessive drooling.
- Shutting down. Lying or standing still and becoming unresponsive, even to their owner.
- Trembling or shaking.
- Cowering. Getting low and "small," hunching over.
- Attention-seeking. Attempts to be near you, "obsessing" over access to you.
- Hypervigilance. Excessively searching, watching and monitoring the environment.
- Hyper-arousal. Inability to relax, constantly moving.

The extent to which a dog shows these behaviors—once in a while, in certain situations or almost all the time—will be a clue as to whether you're dealing with situational or generalized (chronic) anxiety.

Dogs with anxiety need an owner who's willing to do whatever they can to make a predictable environment for their dog. Owners of anxious dogs also need to constantly monitor their pet for changes in body language and behavior that might indicate the need to intervene or change the situation.

What Causes Anxiety in Dogs?

There are a lot of reasons a dog may be anxious. Research suggests that dogs, like people, are impacted by not only their genetics but also their environment, development and learning experiences.

GENETICS A dog's genetic makeup, based on his breed or his parents or both, may play a significant role in how a dog is likely to develop. For example, a dog whose parents were fearful of other dogs is more likely to be fearful of other dogs as well.

LIFE EXPERIENCES AND DEVELOPMENT Early life experiences such as maternal care, puppyhood development, socialization and relationship building all affect the future behavior of a dog.

TRAUMATIC EVENT(S) Dogs that have experienced something traumatic, especially during the critical socialization period, are more likely to be anxious in the future and develop significant behavioral concerns.

LACK OF SOCIALIZATION Early socialization experiences affect how a dog will perceive their world. The adage "Use it or lose it" applies here too: a dog that learned good coping skills in puppyhood will lose those skills in adulthood if they're not consistently practiced.

How Can You Help a Dog with Anxiety?

The first thing to do is to ensure you can read the signs of anxiety in your dog and know the contexts in which they become anxious. Many dog owners find it helpful to keep a log or record of their dog's anxious behaviors and what happened right before, during and after those behaviors occurred. With that context, here are some next steps.

> **"Dogs with anxiety need an owner who's willing to do whatever they can to make a predictable environment for their dog.**

MANAGE YOUR DOG'S ENVIRONMENT. You can't always prevent every incident that causes anxiousness, but you can control your dog's exposure to triggers such as strangers, unfamiliar dogs, where you take your walks, how you leave for work each day and so on.

CREATE A DOGGY SAFE SPACE. Dogs, like people, need a safe space as a retreat in order to relax and rest. This is doubly important for a dog that experiences anxiety. Find a space in your house that your dog can access freely and where they won't be bothered. Furnish the area with comfortable bedding and toys your dog loves. If your dog loves the cooling air of a fan, turn one on and use it as a way to create soothing white noise.

MAINTAIN A RELAXING HOME ENVIRONMENT. We often don't consider how hectic our home life can be for dogs. For a dog that has anxiety issues, being in a home environment that's busy and noisy can cause a lot more stress. Consider ways you can create more calm for your pet, like reducing the number of visitors you have or moving the dog's food bowl to a quiet, private spot. Avoid taking your dog to locations that are crowded or unpredictable. Your dog may also find certain scent sprays and diffusers comforting.

CALL A PROFESSIONAL FOR A BEHAVIORAL CONSULTATION. Anxiety can be a complex and debilitating issue, so if your dog has severe or pervasive anxiety you'll benefit from working with a professional. He or she can help you create an effective, positive reinforcement-based plan that incorporates desensitization and counterconditioning. You can locate a qualified professional through the IAABC's consultant finder.

You may also read about vests, beds, and other products advertised to help your dog handle anxiety. To the extent that any of these tools help create a calm space for your dog to retreat to, they might be helpful. But the best way to help your dog is by creating an environment that eliminates stressors that might trigger your dog's anxiousness.

Where Can You Get Help?

"If you don't know how to proceed, please reach out to a

positive-reinforcement-based trainer who can help you understand and truly address your pet's anxiety," Pachel says. "The long-term goal should be to focus on teaching coping strategies that your pet can use in those stressful situations."

A helpful training and behavior program will focus on reducing the exposure to potential triggers (through good management practices), creating new, positive emotional responses (through desensitization and counter-conditioning) and teaching the dog effective coping skills.

If your dog has severe anxiety, it's likely your veterinarian will recommend prescription medication in combination with a positive reinforcement training program. But for dogs that only sometimes need a little extra help at specific times, you can try an over-the-counter anxiety treat product like Composure treats, but be sure to talk to your vet first before introducing anything new to your dog's body.

There's a lot of information you can find on the internet, but it can be tough to find quality resources when you don't know what to look for. There are tips online on how to recognize canine body language and signs of anxiety. Books focused on understanding your dog's emotions and how to ensure your dog is happy are also helpful in addressing anxiety concerns.

WHY YOUR DOG FOLLOWS YOU EVERYWHERE

From the living room to the bedroom to the kitchen and the bathroom, our dogs are right behind us. We examine the reasons why your pooch always wants to tag along

BY HAYLEE BERGELAND, CPDT-KA, CBCC-KA, RBT

APPARENTLY, WE HUMANS NEED a buddy beside us when we're doing the laundry, changing the sheets, searching for the phone charger and, of course, during bathroom breaks. At least according to our dogs. Maybe they think we need their support, even as we are reaching for the toilet paper roll they chewed on yesterday. Privacy? What's that?

Despite what dog owners are often told (thanks Google!), this behavior has nothing to do with your dog being a pack animal or your dog trying to "steal" your space. Dogs, like people, are social animals and they enjoy the company of their loved ones. They love it so much that at times they will endure your dirty bathroom (don't look at mine!) just to be with you.

REASONS YOUR DOG MIGHT FOLLOW YOU EVERYWHERE

Human-Animal Bond After so many years of selective breeding, dogs are truly man's best friend. If you have a close relationship with your dog built on trust and understanding, your physical presence is crucial to maintaining that beautiful companionship. Plus, positive interactions with humans have been shown to raise oxytocin levels in our dogs. So, being near their BFF actually feels good, too.

Boredom After being alone for hours, or when there are no birds out the window to obsess over, our dogs become increasingly bored and require good enrichment. If you don't provide it, trust me, they will find ways to entertain themselves. A bored dog may also find that if they continue to follow you around, you will finally get the hint that it is walkies time.

Anxiousness Dogs experience nervousness, fear and anxiety in a way that is very similar to how we feel it. And just like us, when our dogs become anxious they may want to be near someone that makes them feel safe and secure. For many anxious dogs, separation from the person they are bonded with only adds to their stress.

Reinforcement If you and your dog have a history of positive reinforcement training together, and your dog knows that you provide access to all things fun and tasty, your presence alone is a solid indicator of good things to come. Plus, it's not hard to figure out that when you're making a snack in the kitchen it might equal delicious crumbs on the floor.

Breed Some breeds, in particular those that have been bred for centuries to work alongside a human, are hardwired to stay near their person. The herding group is a good example of this. Herding dogs have learned to pay very close attention to their owner's cues, wait for new information, and be ready to perform a specific task (like gather the sheep). Other breed groups, such as the working group, have been selectively bred to be on-the-job with their owners.

Unmet Needs or Medical issues Sometimes we just don't pick up on the not-so-subtle hints that our dogs need to go outside. Dogs that all of a sudden become "clingy" may need a potty break. Dogs who aren't feeling well or have an underlying medical issue, might suddenly begin to follow you around more.

WHEN SHOULD YOU BE CONCERNED?

Although it can get annoying, even a tad creepy, the majority of the time your dog wants to follow you is nothing to be concerned about. However, if your dog obsessively following you is a new behavior, that may indicate they need to be seen by a veterinarian or behavior consultant.

It's important to pay extra-close attention to canine body language and communication. If you notice your dog's following-you-around behavior includes signs of stress, you should seek help from a certified behavior consultant or positive reinforcement trainer. A tense-looking body, vocalizations such as whining or barking or the inability to settle down would all suggest issues of fear or even anxiety.

If you find the behavior came on suddenly, there could be an underlying health issue. Moving slowly or groaning when lying down, sensitivity to touch or changes in behavior like not eating or issues pottying indicate a need to be seen by your vet right away.

Dogs, like people, are social animals and they enjoy the company of their loved ones.

Why Dogs Bark and How You Can Control It

Moving beyond "Will you please be quiet, please?"

BY LISA RADOSTA, DVM, DACVB, AND AUSTIN CANNON

EVER WONDER WHY your dog barks so much? He barks when there are people walking by. He barks when he wants you to play with him or take him out. He barks when you leave the house. Or he barks at night. Sometimes you appreciate the barking when you are at home alone and he alerts you to a strange sound. Sometimes though, it might be nice to have some peace and quiet instead of knowing about every squirrel that crosses the backyard.

Barking serves many purposes in the dog-human relationship, but almost all barks can be boiled down to one thing: communication. Once you figure out what your dog is trying to say, the fixes are pretty straightforward.

Why Is Your Dog Barking?

Barking is a normal behavior that can communicate many different emotional states or needs. Some of the most common reasons for barking include:

- Fear, anxiety, stress (storm phobia, noise phobia, separation anxiety, strangers in the house)
- To alert the family to a perceived threat (people, dogs walking by)
- Display frustration (squirrels just out of reach)
- To get attention for play, petting, to go outside, or come back into the house
- Pain or discomfort

While dogs bark to communicate many different emotional states or needs, what keeps them barking is pretty straightforward: reinforcement. Reinforcement is the scientific word for reward. It is the jet fuel that keeps the behavior going. If your dog has a full tank (lots of reinforcement) the jet can go across the world. If you can control or eliminate the reinforcement, your dog's jet will run out of fuel and he will be quiet as a church mouse. Well, maybe not that quiet, but he will bark a lot less.

Do Dogs Ever Get Tired of Barking?

Eventually, but most dog owners will tell you it'll take awhile. They'll get frustrated because they think you aren't listening to them. As the barking continues, they'll eventually get physically tired.

"If they feel like no one is listening to the bark, other dogs included, they may become mentally exhausted, but that doesn't mean barking itself makes them feel tired," says Haylee Bergeland, CPDT-KA, CBCC-KA, RBT. While it might be tempting to throw on the noise-canceling headphones and go on with your day, the first step to getting them to quiet down is to figure out why they're barking. Then you can work on it from there. Example: if your pup barks at every person, thing or animal passing by your window, interrupting your WFH video chats, maybe consider closing the curtains, suggests Bergeland.

"If a need is met, the reason for the barking is addressed, they will stop," she says.

Same goes for when your dog barks to go outside: let her outside! Don't yell or punish your dog for barking. It does nothing to address why she is barking, it's mean, and it could even make her bark more, Bergeland says.

Instead of punishment, try offering your dog something else to do instead of bark. Bergeland says you can train your dog to do something instead of bark: bringing you a toy or sitting down in front of you, for example. If that doesn't work, make it impossible for your dog to bark

If your dog reacts badly to guests, put him in another room before visitors arrive, then introduce him later. The sight and sound of someone other than a family member at the door can be an intense situation for a dog.

by giving them a toy to chew or perhaps a peanut-butter filled Kong. Doesn't that sound good?

Do Some Dogs Bark More Than Others?

Indeed! Your terriers will be pretty vocal because they were bred to alert their owners to small critters, Bergeland says. Same for herding dogs and hounds—that's how they let their owners know when they've found prey or identified a threat.

But that doesn't mean your poodle is gonna stay quiet. (Can confirm as a poodle owner. They bark plenty.)

"Dogs in general—meaning all breeds—bark, because over the span of evolving around humans, barking became a way to communicate on a larger, louder scale," Bergeland says.

Are You Reinforcing Barking?

Dogs are smart creatures and don't do things that aren't reinforcing to them. For instance:

- Your dog barks at you to take him out. You get up from your comfy chair and walk him. Barking reinforced.
- Your dog barks at you after dropping a ball at your feet. You toss the ball. Barking reinforced.
- Your dog barks at neighbors going by the house. The people leave. (They were walking by anyway.) Barking reinforced.

All that reinforcement keeps your dog's barking behavior strong. The more that he does it, the more he will do it.

This discussion wouldn't be complete without giving special attention to the barking that's exhibited when your dog is fearful, anxious or stressed. Very often, when dogs bark at strangers or new things on walks, it's because those things are scary. This type of barking is unique in that the reinforcement isn't always under your control. Also, using the incorrect technique to try to change this type of barking can backfire, pushing your dog into a place where he will bite someone. Because of this, the fix for this type of barking is a little more complex. More on that later.

How to Stop a Dog from Barking

You want to stop your dog from barking at night. You want your dog to stop barking at other dogs. You want your dog to stop barking at the window. Follow the tips below to help your dog to know when he can bark and when he should be quiet.

TAKE A LONG HARD LOOK IN THE MIRROR. Yes, we are starting with your behavior. You cannot have it both ways. You cannot love that your dog barks at people who approach your house but get upset with him when he barks at people when they come into the house. He is not a mind reader. He doesn't know which people are friends or foes. He may be fearful, anxious or stressed (remember when we talked about how that emotional state is more complex to treat?), which will cause him to be less responsive to you. Modify your expectations to be realistic. What would you expect of a 2-year-old child? That is an appropriate expectation for your dog. What have you truly taught him? Only those behaviors that he knows very well can be expected to be performed. If you didn't teach it, don't expect it.

AVOID SITUATIONS WHERE YOUR DOG MIGHT BARK, BUT SHOULDN'T. Avoidance is easy, free and highly effective. It is the first step for lots of dogs regardless of why they bark. Here's how avoidance might help your dog in the most common situations:

- To stop your dog from barking at strangers: put her in a separate room before strangers come over.
- To stop your dog from barking at the window: block off the windows or that part of the house.
- To stop your dog from barking at you for attention: ignore him and/or walk away.

TEACH AN ALTERNATE BEHAVIOR. Everyone is focused on correcting their dog's behavior. Let's focus on teaching your dog what he can do to earn reinforcement. For instance, instead of barking, you might direct your dog to go to a bed and lie down, be quiet, or hold a toy and go to another room. You can find easy-to-implement, effective techniques on how to train these behaviors in a positive way in the book *From Fearful to Fear Free* by Marty Becker, Lisa Radosta, Wailani Sung and Mikkel Becker.

DISTRACT YOUR DOG. This is another easy, inexpensive technique that works to stop a dog from barking. When your dog is barking, get his attention by shaking a treat bag or introducing his favorite toy. Keep him occupied, away from the thing at which he is barking, until it is gone. Wait! Won't you reinforce the barking? Will your dog learn to bark for the toy or treat? Well, it is more complex than that, but let's just say, maybe. However, the barking that your dog does for the toy or treat in this situation will be short-lived and easy to control unlike the all-day barking he does as he lies on the back of the couch staring out the window.

DON'T GO FOR PUNISHMENT. Yelling, grabbing dogs and shocking them with electric collars isn't necessary and isn't the most effective way to get your dog to listen to you and stop barking. If your dog has those special exception emotional states (fear, anxiety and stress) you will make his behavior worse, which is not what we want to do!

When Should You Get Pro Help to Stop a Dog from Barking?

Dogs are voiceless. They cannot tell you when they don't feel well. Any changes in your dog's behavior, even if they come on slowly, should prompt a physical examination. Schedule a visit with your veterinarian to rule out physical causes for your dog's vocalizations.

If you aren't making progress with simple fixes like the ones outlined in this article, you may need help from a positive reinforcement trainer. Board certified veterinary behaviorists are another professional option you can investigate. These pros are essentially veterinary psychiatrists. They are experts in all things behavior and are veterinarians, so they understand how pain, discomfort and disease can cause the signs that you are seeing. The American College of Veterinary Behaviorists can tell you more about how a veterinary behaviorist might help you, or help you find one in your area.

What If My Dog's Barking Is Due to Fear, Anxiety or Stress?

These emotional states are unique. If you think your dog has any of these emotional states, go to your veterinarian and if necessary ask for a referral for a board certified veterinary behaviorist. If treated correctly, the barking and the fear can go bye-bye. If not, the consequences can be lifelong and very negative.

Barking is normal. Expect of your dog only what he can give, try to find out what he is trying to tell you, and teach him what he needs to know to bark only when necessary.

What Does It Mean When a Dog Has a Strong Prey Drive?

This may be a matter of ability and desire

BY HAYLEE BERGELAND, CPDT-KA, CBCC-KA, RBT

OUR DOGS OFTEN do things that we have a difficult time understanding. They dig, they chew, they eat garbage, they nip at our heels or chase our cats. They often leave us scratching our heads, looking for answers to explain their canine antics. When we don't know how to explain why our dogs do such things, and those things make us concerned, we might chalk it up to a commonly used term, prey drive. But what is prey drive, really?

Unfortunately, there is no easy definition or explanation. I know, I know, it figures. But labeling behaviors in dogs is a complicated business, and doing so without caution can lead to a lot of frustration, for both you and your dog.

What Could the Term Prey Drive Mean?

Commonly, when we refer to prey drive we are talking about a dog's ability, and desire, to find, pursue and catch prey. In some circles, prey drive is synonymous with high energy and a general desire to perform behaviors or "work."

So let's break the term down a little. When you talk about prey, there are a lot of different things you could be referring to. Does the dog want to find, pursue and catch an animal? A toy? A piece of food? What does the dog want to do with it? Karen B. London, PhD, a certified applied animal behaviorist and certified professional dog trainer, asks, "Does it mean a drive to run, to chase, to catch something, to bite it, to kill it, or any combination of these?" The answers to those questions vary with the situation.

Now the word "drive." From an ethological perspective (meaning looking at the behavior of animals in their "natural world"), prey drive isn't really a thing and can be confused with predatory behavior. The concept of "drive" can be summed up as motivation or desire, which fluctuates from one situation to the next. For example, if you just ate a huge meal and then someone asks you to walk to a local eatery for an ice cream, you likely will have little, if any, motivation (or drive) to do so. However, if you haven't eaten a sweet snack all day, you may be much more excited to go for that walk.

Generally, here's how I think we're safest using the term prey drive: when we are attributing prey drive to an entire breed, we are referring to a predisposition to hunt, pursue and capture prey, which can be natural doggie behaviors that many breeds have as a genetic predisposition. I tend to avoid including "chasing" under the term prey drive because most dogs enjoy a good game of chase but don't necessarily want to "capture"; when the chasing fun is done, they are content to do something else. For example, herding breeds, like the Australian cattle dog or Border collie, love to chase and nip ankles, but their goal isn't to snare quarry. I have an Australian shepherd (Aussie) and a borzoi. My Aussie *looooves* to chase things, including us and his canine buddies, but he stops the second the movement ends. My borzoi, on the other hand, once very nearly caught a rabbit as it fled through a small hole in our fence. I doubt he would have known what to do with the rabbit if he had caught it, but the desire to try was certainly apparent. Both of them live peacefully inside my home with my two cats, which surprises many people who believe a cat could be prey to a very "houndy" dog.

> **"*If you're considering adopting a dog whose breed is known for having a strong predisposition for prey drive behaviors, make sure you do extensive research.*"**

Owners are often surprised and frustrated by behaviors associated with hunting, especially chasing behaviors, and when they think of these actions as prey drive they may become concerned their dog has a serious issue, such as aggression.

Does My Dog Have a High Prey Drive? And Should I Worry?

Using the term prey drive doesn't necessarily describe a specific dog's personality but instead labels a lot of different behaviors or actions happening at a specific moment. What is important is the context: What are you seeing? When is it happening? Prey drive is the sum of lots of different behaviors occurring together in a certain context.

Breeds that have been systematically bred to pursue, chase or hunt are more likely to exhibit behaviors associated with the term prey drive. For underprepared owners, not recognizing and addressing these potential behaviors in their dog's breed could lead to trouble. For instance, owners should understand it is possible their rat terrier may capture and kill (and maybe eat) unsuspecting chipmunks, or the owner of a saluki should understand their dog may suddenly take off after a rabbit. Careful consideration should be taken when introducing any dog to your home, especially a breed that could have a genetic predisposition to these sorts of behaviors.

"The bottom line is that every dog is an individual, but breeding makes a difference. While all dogs have it in them to chase things, and some even to bite or kill another animal, certain breeds

The borzoi hound was developed as a hunting companion, with an emphasis on speed. Like most sight hounds, borzoi have a high prey drive.

have been designed to do this more than others," says Irith Bloom, CPDT-KSA, CBCC-KA, CDBC, CSAT, KPA CTP, VSPDT, CBATI.

If you're considering adopting a dog whose breed is known for having a strong predisposition for prey drive behaviors, make sure you do extensive research, planning and preparation before you bring the dog home. Speak with a reputable breeder, a licensed veterinarian and a certified professional dog trainer. Hang out with an owner, observe the dog breed around other dogs, people and other animals. The more informed you are, the better chance you have of selecting a canine companion well-suited to your lifestyle.

On the other hand, just because your dog loves to chase or sniff out and pursue local critters on your walks doesn't mean you need to be concerned he has aggressive tendencies or will be difficult to live with. You will want to observe any such behaviors in as many contexts as you safely can before making any behavior labels. When your dog is doing something that concerns you or you are having a difficult time managing your dog, it is best to seek the help of a veterinary behaviorist or certified animal behavior consultant.

Of course, sound management is always your best first step when it comes to dealing with doggie behaviors. Through the use of positive reinforcement, you can teach a dog to ignore things that might normally catch their eye and instead pay attention to you, or to comply with behaviors more suitable for your needs, like following the commands "Come," "Stay" or "Leave it."

Cultivate Happiness

You might be surprised at how easy it is to improve your four-legged best friend's mood

BY HAYLEE BERGELAND, CPDT-KA, CBCC-KA, RBT

DOGS DO SO MUCH TO ENRICH OUR LIVES. THEY MAKE US laugh, they provide company, they entertain us and they don't judge our life choices (thankfully). They can truly be our best friends, and we want to do our best to return the favor.

From the day we bring home our dogs, we look for ways to entertain them and make sure they're healthy. But there's a lot more we can do to

ensure they are truly happy, living their best dog life right alongside us. One key to their happiness starts with their ability to decide for themselves.

How to Tell If Your Dog Is Happy

While happiness is pretty subjective—in humans and pets—we know that happy dogs engage in a variety of activities.

Sometimes a happy dog is one that is playing, other times a happy dog is one that is napping. "Since dogs are social animals, a happy dog will usually have a good balance of activity on his or her own, social activities with others in the home, and rest," says Irith Bloom, KPA-CTP, CDBC, CPDT-KSA, director of training at The Sophisticated Dog, LLC.

When a dog is happy, or enjoying the activity they are doing, you will see it in their canine communication and body language. Differences in breed appearances can muddy the body-language waters, but there are signals you can watch for.

A HAPPY DOG'S FACE WILL SHOW: relaxed facial muscles, brow is smooth and relaxed, eyes appear "soft," ears are loose, a relaxed, slightly opened mouth, lips appear wrinkle-free.

A HAPPY DOG'S BODY WILL SHOW: running with a bouncy gate, relaxed body muscles, affiliative behavior (wanting to be close) or soliciting attention, tail is loose and hanging naturally.

"To ensure your dog is happy, give your dog a lot of options for ways to keep busy. Food toys, chew toys, walks, training time with you and playtime with you are all part of a happy life. Dogs who get too little of these types of activity can get bored and depressed," Bloom says.

If you're concerned about your dog's behavior, or she appears less happy than usual, see your vet to rule out physical health issues.

How to Tell If Your Dog Is Not Happy

The things that make us humans happy are not necessarily the same things that will make our dogs happy. While we may enjoy going to parties, hanging out at a festival or going to a new friend's house for dinner, dogs don't. Not only is it unfair to force our likes on our fur babies, but it can create a stressed dog instead of a happy one.

Learning to recognize the signs of an unhappy dog can be a game of opposites. A tired dog might be worn out from having fun—or may actually be stressed. They may avoid food—or gobble it down too quickly. They may appear sluggish—or they may be overly rambunctious. And these are just a few examples. Learning the signs and signals exhibited by your own dog is crucial to recognizing their unhappiness.

While this isn't an exhaustive list, here are some signals.

A STRESSED DOG'S FACE MIGHT SHOW: tight, closed mouth, ears back and tight against head or alert, whites of eyes that can be easily seen, avoidance of eye contact, grimace appearance on face, wrinkled skin around the mouth.

A STRESSED DOG'S BODY MIGHT SHOW: stiff body posture, tail tucked or very slowly wagging, hackles up (hair on back), weight shifted forward, cowering, trembling or shaking.

> **"A happy dog will usually have a good balance of activity on his or her own, social activities with others in the home, and rest."**
>
> —IRITH BLOOM

Choices Make Any Dog Happy

Whether your dog is just a puppy or a distinguished senior, every dog has a hierarchy of needs. But just meeting those basic needs isn't enough to make your dog happy. One crucial thing that dog parents often forget: dogs need the ability to make choices for themselves.

Choice goes beyond just choosing which dog treat they like best or which squeaky toy will come home from the pet store. Choice involves letting a dog decide when, how, who, where and what. It gives your dog the ability to say no, which many dog owners forget to give their dog a chance to say. There are several ways pet parents can offer choices to their dog, including easy-to-incorporate options like when to go for walks or when to play.

"It's important to give your dog permission to make choices," Bloom says. "Often, dogs don't have a choice about when or how they are petted. Most dogs also don't get to choose when and where to walk, or how fast (or slow) to move while on a walk."

5 WAYS TO MAKE YOUR DOG HAPPY

Here's what you can do to give your dog choices and increase his or her happiness—and make the world a better place for dogs.

THE CHOICE TO REFUSE BEING TOUCHED
Dogs should be allowed to say no to being touched, petted or hugged—and you should respect this decision.

THE CHOICE TO LEAVE A SITUATION
Never force a dog to remain in a scary situation and never restrict a dog's ability to get away from something that makes her or him uncomfortable.

THE CHOICE TO BE IN A SAFE SPACE
Providing a safe, quiet place where no one can bother your dog (like space invaders!) is an important way to keep her or him happy. This space should be available at all times.

THE CHOICE TO REFUSE TRAINING
Positive reinforcement training should always be fun. Sometimes a dog is just too tired or the environment is just too stressful. Your dog should be able to tell you when they feel up to the task, and you need to listen.

THE CHOICE TO SMELL
Dogs experience the world through their noses. On walks and in your backyard, allow your dog time to enjoy sniffing and smelling the surroundings.

Chapter Three

CREATING A MENSA DOG / RULES OF SEPARATION / CREATE A PUPPY SCHEDULE / HOW TO NAIL HOUSEBREAKING / EASIER VET VISITS

TRAINING DAYS

Here's how to communicate and bond with your dog in ways that will make learning new behaviors second nature

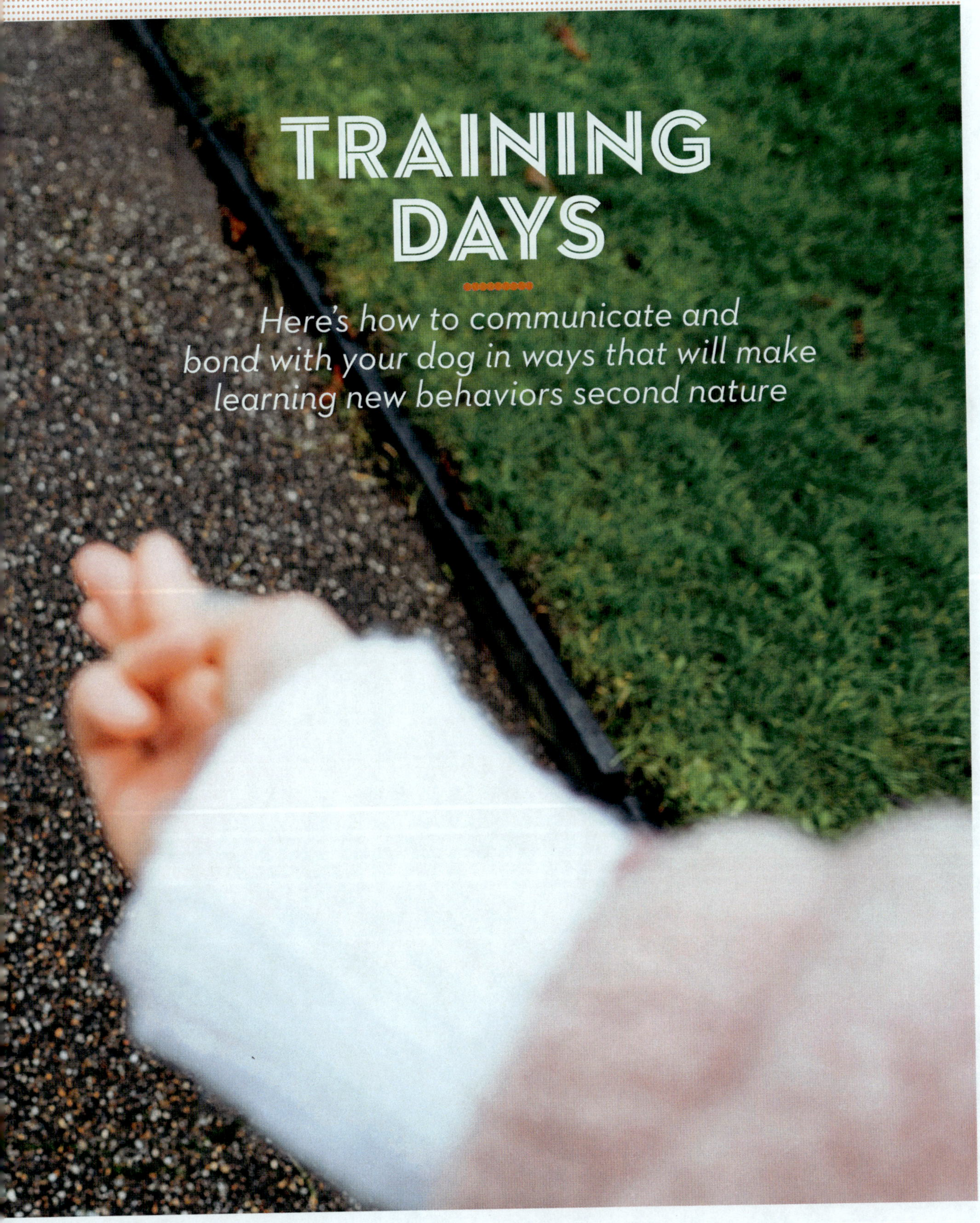

Creating a Mensa Dog

With postive, reward-based training, you just might wind up with the smartest dog on the block

BY KATHERINE ALBRO HOUPT, VMD, PHD, DACVB

YOU HAVE JUST adopted Farley, a 1-year-old mixed-breed dog, and you would like to be sure he fits well in your active household. You have received many suggestions for where to train Farley, but the recommendations all seem to have a different take on how to train a dog. How do you choose which is the best approach for Farley?

Most people would like to have the smartest dog on the block— a Mensa dog. Mensa is an association of people who have scored very high on intelligence tests. So would you like Farley to be a Mensa dog? Are you sure? Some of the most unhappy dog owners are those with very smart dogs who are underemployed. Do you really want a dog who can open any door, knows what taking out the suitcases means, buries the nail clipper and remembers the weak spot in the fence?

For most people, the perfect dog comes when called, drops even the most delicious food when asked, never jumps up on anyone, stays when told and does a few tricks to amuse your guests. And you know what? He doesn't need a PhD to learn these things, and you don't need one to teach him. Here is how to teach your dog tasks that can make your life and his easier—plus, the difference between what you think you're teaching and what the dog thinks you're teaching.

Facts, Not Fiction

"You can't teach an old dog new tricks." That is definitely fiction. Snowy was a 10-year-old Westie who learned to sit at 10 years of age.

Up until that time, for what his owners needed, he was the perfect dog. He never really had to be taught anything. He lived in the country and could roam in the yard that he never left. He jumped in greeting, but jumped in the air, not on people. He taught himself to sit up and beg. The only reason he needed to learn to sit at age 10 is that this was when his life circumstances changed. And guess what? He did learn to sit when asked, demonstrating that, in fact, you can teach an old dog new tricks.

What is true is that dogs learn more slowly in old age, just as humans do. The decline in learning ability (and cognitive function) can be slowed to a great extent in dogs, as in humans, with the right diet and environmental enrichment, especially social enrichment—increased opportunities for interactions with other dogs and people.

The Smartest Dogs

All dogs are smart enough to teach us to provide them with food, water, shelter and, usually, exercise and veterinary care. Which dogs are the smartest? It depends on how you define smart. This is a form of associative learning: the dog learns to associate words with objects. It is a prodigious feat. But what may be more impressive is insightful behavior. We all know that dogs can be sneaky, and recently this was proven in an experiment in which a dog could take a treat from either a dish that made noise when he touched it or from a silent container. If a person was not watching, the dog chose the silent container, thus not alerting the owner. He was being insightful.

So what are the mental abilities of dogs? They can certainly learn to associate objects and also tasks with words. They can match to sample—a task in which the dog is shown one object and then must choose between that object and a novel one; choosing the familiar object is rewarded. For example, if you show a dog a red rubber squirrel and then show him a pile of toys, picking out the red rubber squirrel from the pile is matching to sample. Dogs do not do as well at matching toys with photographs of toys, though.

While it is unlikely that dogs understand geometry, they can make mental maps. If you walk a dog on a leash in an L-shaped path away from a goal (food), when released he will take a shortcut to make his way back to the food. These mental maps persist too. Hide a toy or treat, and he can remember where it was hidden for half an hour.

However, dogs are not so good at barrier problems. If they are inside a V-shaped barrier, they can figure out how to run around the barrier to get a reward on the outside of the V. But if they are outside the V, they have trouble understanding that they must run around the barrier to get the reward inside the V.

What Is Learning?

Learning is defined as acquiring knowledge by instruction. At its most basic, it's a multistep physical process involving electrical impulses, release of chemicals and formation of proteins.

Most dogs, especially Mensa dogs, learn quickly that "Sit" means a treat is coming and will stop complying if you don't have a treat. You can fix that.

Information is received by nerve cells that send an electrical impulse to the end of the nerve, where neurochemicals are released and stimulate the next nerve. When this process is repeated enough times, the nerve will form new proteins and eventually grow new pathways. In other words, your dog's brain actually changes as he learns. The more often a given combination of nerves is stimulated, the more likely the behavior will occur in response to that specific stimulus. The next time you say "Sit" and your dog sits, think about all the processes that were involved in forming that memory.

In fact, your dog is learning all the time—when you specifically teach him and when you don't. Remember when, as a puppy, he stuck his nose in a candle flame? He learned to avoid fire with no assistance from you. Similarly, he learned on his own that there really wasn't another dog in the mirror. Every day, every walk you take your dog on, he is constantly learning. It doesn't matter how young or old he is.

The following are some ways in which dogs learn.

Classical Conditioning

Almost everyone knows about Pavlov's dogs. The principle Pavlov discovered still applies today, and we can make use of it. Ivan Pavlov was actually studying salivation and won his Nobel Prize not for psychology but for his study of how the intestinal tract works. In the process of collecting saliva from his dogs, however, he realized that the dogs were salivating before they tasted any meat.

Salivating when tasting meat is an unconditioned response, meaning it does not have to be learned. It happens automatically. Pavlov's dogs had learned a conditioned response: they associated the preparations for the experiment with the meat they were fed, and responded as if they had tasted the meat. Pavlov found that not only the sight of meat but also the sound of a bell would cause the dogs to salivate if the sound had regularly occurred just before the meat was presented to the dog. This kind of

Does the name Pavlov ring a bell? The work he did in the 1890s still informs our understanding of conditioning.

conditioning—where an unconditioned response (in Pavlov's experiment, salivating) can be elicited by pairing it with an unrelated stimulus (ringing a bell)—is classical conditioning.

This same sort of conditioned response is the basis for a training method called "clicker training." Clicker training is an increasingly popular way to train dogs. The clicker is a plastic toylike device with a metal strip that makes a quick, clear, consistent and distinctive clicking sound when pressed, making it ideal for this type of training.

The principle behind clicker training is classical conditioning: associate a sound (in this case a click) with an unconditioned response (the taste of a delicious treat). It will take only a few minutes for your dog to form the association: click means treat. The process of creating that association is simple enough. Give a single click, then immediately give or toss a treat to your dog. Do that about twenty times, and he will have formed the association that a click means the treat is coming. The click now becomes a reward all by itself, because the sound lets the dog predict that a treat will soon appear.

Now you can use this technique to teach your dog almost anything, using another form of learning—operant conditioning. You simply click the instant your dog does the behavior you are trying to teach, and then follow up with the treat. The click means "What you just did is exactly what I wanted, and now your reward is on the way."

A hand signal denotes the exact moment your dog does something for which he earns a reinforcer, or a treat. Pick one gesture and stick to it, marking the behavior when you see it.

Making a Learned Behavior "Stick"

Most dogs, especially Mensa dogs, learn quickly that "Sit" means a treat is coming, and they will quickly stop complying if you don't have a treat. The technical term is that the response will be extinguished. To avoid this problem, you have to teach your dog to be a gambler, like someone feeding those Las Vegas slot machines over and over, hoping for the big win.

That is, you want your dog to keep offering the learned response, even if he doesn't get a treat every time, in hopes that eventually the reward will appear. To turn him into a gambler, you can give him a reward every other time he sits (only after he learns "Sit" reliably and is getting a reward every time). But every other time is too easy to predict, so you'll have to start offering rewards randomly—every second time, every tenth, every fifth and so on. He can't predict when the reward will come, so he'll keep offering the response in hopes that next time will get him the payoff.

This is called a "variable ratio of reinforcement," which means the frequency of the reward (the rate of reinforcement) varies. Animals can learn to repeat actions hundreds of times for a single reward using this technique. Nini, a cairn terrier, was taught to jump into the car on request for a treat. She lived to 16 and would still jump in the car when asked, even though eventually she got a treat only about every 14th time she was asked to jump in.

How Do We Begin?

Let's try to teach Farley to sit. First, the environment should be conducive to learning. That means no distractions—no squirrels outside the window, no loud music or other dogs barking. You should not be distracted either—no watching TV out of the corner of your eye. For learning to take place, both you and your dog need a calm, focused environment.

To teach "Sit," hold a piece of delicious food right in front of his nose, then pass your hand back between his ears. He should put his nose up, and when his nose goes up, his rump goes down. When his rump touches the floor, say "Sit" and give him the food. Don't say "Sit" until he starts to squat, because he has no idea what that word means until you have paired his action of sitting and the word at least a dozen times. Once he has learned to sit in that nice quiet environment, it is time to help him generalize by asking him to sit in other places and in more distracting situations. (Generalizing is when an animal learns that after a behavior is established in one particular environment or with one particular person, it should also occur in all other environments with everyone.) When you do that, you have a chance of controlling his behavior even when he is aroused or frightened.

Next let's teach Farley to lie down. There are ways to force a dog to lie down by pulling his front legs forward or to trick him into lying down by holding food on the floor. But the easiest way is to wait for him to lie down spontaneously and then reinforce that behavior.

If you're using a clicker, he already knows what the clicker means (he did exactly the right behavior, and now a treat is on the way!), so you can sit back and wait for him to lie down. Just as he does, mark the moment with a click. Then you have a few seconds to toss him a treat. You don't have to say anything—and in fact, you should wait until he is repeatedly lying down before pairing his action with words and a hand signal.

Why use both a word and a hand signal? Dogs are visual animals and communicate primarily by reading body posture. Research done by veterinary behaviorist Daniel Mills suggests that dogs seem to respond better to hand signals than to words. Also, hand signals can enhance your elderly dog's quality of life. Hopefully, your dog will live well into his teens. If he does, he'll probably lose some of his hearing ability, at which time he will respond only to the request he perceives—a hand signal. Still, the spoken word can save your dog's life. What if he's running toward a squirrel that's on the other side of the street? He won't see your hand signal as he runs toward the squirrel, but he can hear you calling and will lie down rather than dart out into a busy street, avoiding pitfalls and staying on track.

Getting Angry

Farley is not too good at the recall, and today he heads for the neighbor's house when you are in a hurry to leave. You call and call and he ignores you. Finally, you follow him and call again. He comes to you, and as soon as he gets to you, you begin to berate him. "Bad dog, bad Farley."

Poor Farley is very confused; he came, but you scolded him when he did. You may even have jerked his collar. He thought he knew what "Come" meant, but now it means "Come and be scolded by a really angry person." The next time you call him, he may not come, or he might come with head and tail down.

It is very hard to keep your temper when a dog does not do what you ask. But you must remain calm and relaxed if you want a well-trained dog. This is true of all the behaviors you teach your dog, but especially "Come."

Food-Reward Pitfalls

Often when dog owners are asked during a behavioral consultation to demonstrate their dog's response to "Sit" and "Down," many say, "Oh, he'll only do that if I have food." But your dog should comply with a request every time you ask, whether you have food or not. What's wrong?

You have to reward the dog if you expect him to do something for you. He is no more likely to work for no salary than you are. But once he has made the association between a word and an action, you do not have to reward him every single time. In fact, you shouldn't. Never knowing when the reward will come will keep your dog "gambling" in hopes of the big payoff. Remember our discussion of variable reinforcement (rewarding a well-learned behavior intermittently instead of continuously after each repetition of the behavior).

Failure to Generalize

What if your dog does very well at obedience school and in your living room, but he doesn't seem to understand your requests when you visit other people or while you're walking? This is likely a failure to generalize his learning from one environment to another. Practice in a variety of situations—and with various distractions—to help him generalize his skills.

Building Confidence

Through the thoughtful use of counterconditioning you can help develop your fearful pet's tenacity

BY HAYLEE BERGELAND, CPDT-KA, CBCC-KA, RBT

WHETHER YOUR GOAL is to help your dog overcome the scariness of vacuums, or you want your puppy to feel better about the loud sounds that accompany most holiday activities, counterconditioning combined with desensitization and positive reinforcement goes a long way toward helping your pet build confidence and feel better about the human world.

Minimizing fear, like many others goals of training, can be achieved through conditioning. Whenever you see the word conditioning, think "learning." Our animals learn by association and through interaction with their environment.

Classical conditioning (or respondent conditioning), simply put, happens when two things are repeatedly paired together to create a new response (behavior) or association. The learner, in this case, your pet, learns to associate one thing with the other. One of those things already has meaning and natural value (like food) and the other is totally neutral.

Classical conditioning occurs naturally, or involuntarily. For example, your dog learns that the sound of your keys jingling means they might go for a ride or that the sound of the refrigerator opening might mean an opportunity for a quick snack. Building an association between a marker and a reinforcer, like the sound of a clicker and the delivery of treats (a reinforcer), is a really common and very helpful example of how we can use classical conditioning to teach our animals all sorts of things.

What Is Counterconditioning and Desensitization?

Counterconditioning, on the other hand, is the process of replacing a feeling and response (behavior) that was learned through conditioning. We can help our pets to have a new emotional response to something that is causing them to feel stressed or scared, but we need to be able to recognize when our pets are feeling fear or experiencing stress or anxiety, so that we can identify what we can change and how. Recognizing the subtle signs of a dog that is stressed, and when and why (context), is critical to being able to use counterconditioning and desensitization effectively.

Say your dog is afraid of new dogs they see on walks around your neighborhood. If we want to teach our dogs to feel better about other dogs, every time they see another dog on a walk, you would give them their absolute favorite reinforcer. Food (like treats) is often the best reinforcer for this because it is easy to give and our animals want it in many contexts. (Just like me!) If they eat the food and it tastes good and makes them feel better, and you do this every time they see other dogs, eventually your dog will learn that seeing other dogs during walkies predicts awesome nummies.

With repeated pairings of favorite reinforcers and new dogs, your dog will begin to have a different emotional response to the sight of new dogs. Now new dogs make your dog feel happy and excited instead of scared. Of course, this really only applies to other dogs on walks and seeing them. Being near them and interacting with them is a whole new ball game. If your dog is also scared of new dogs in other contexts, like say at the dog park or in puppy class, you will need to apply these same practices in those situations, too. And sometimes the most practical choice is just to use good management. If your dog is afraid of strange dogs, then instead of walking past many dogs at the park, take a new route home and avoid the park altogether.

Counterconditioning is used alongside desensitization; animal professionals often refer to these techniques as CC & DS. Zazie Todd, PhD, of Companion Animal Psychology, says, "Desensitization means very gradual exposure to the scary thing, starting at a very low level and building up very slowly. It should be systematic, which means you have a plan to build up gradually. At every step of the way, your dog should be happy and comfortable."

Systematic desensitization requires a lot of thoughtful planning and preparation. Think of it like baby steps; working at your pet's level enables your dog to make choices that keep him calm along the way. Your goal is for your pet to experience brief moments of the scary thing in a safe environment while they feel emotionally secure, and then gradually increase exposure. Go too far or too fast and you wind up overwhelming your pet, which is extremely uncomfortable and scary and only makes matters much worse.

The 4th of July and New Year's Eve present big opportunities to use desensitization. "Suppose your dog is afraid of fireworks," says Todd. "You find a recording of firework sounds. You can't start by playing the sounds at anywhere near normal volume, because you already know that frightens your dog. Instead, you start at a really low volume—maybe even barely audible. Then gradually over time, always making sure your dog is comfortable, you keep turning up the volume a notch. Then another notch. And so on. Over time, assuming you get it right, your dog will learn to tolerate the sounds."

Tips on Counterconditioning and Desensitization

1. TIMING IS EVERYTHING!

Returning to the example of a dog scared of seeing other dogs on walks: If you deliver the awesome treat too late, and your dog is now feeling scared at the sight of the strange dog, the treat may not be enough to help them. If you are too early in giving the treat and you give it before your dog even sees the other dog, then the treat doesn't get associated with the presence of the other dog.

2. CHOOSING THE RIGHT REINFORCER IS CRUCIAL FOR SUCCESS

For instance, you won't change how your dog feels about other dogs if you give them just regular ol' kibble pieces right after they have eaten dinner. In that scenario, the kibble is probably pretty boring in comparison to getting upset

Turn the vacuum cleaner on in a room far from your dog so that the sound is muffled. You may need to close the door to the room. Every few days move the vacuum slightly closer until it can be left running at a reasonable distance from your pup.

over other dogs, plus your dog's belly might already be full. You need to be flexible and willing to choose the right treats or thing that is most reinforcing to your individual pet. Foods like cheese, pieces of lunch meat, hot dog bits and even liver or tripe can be great options for dogs, but you might find your dog also wants space or more distance between them and the scary thing, too. Reinforcers are determined by the learner and can change depending on the context.

3. YOU HAVE TO BE CONSISTENT

To change how your pet feels about scary things you must give those amazing reinforcers every single time the scary thing occurs. You can't just do it randomly and expect your dog to feel differently in a day or two. It . . . takes . . . *time.* If you have a pet who is experiencing serious behavioral concerns, work with a certified professional animal trainer, certified animal behavior consultant or veterinary behaviorist.

Whether you're hoping to help your scared dog feel more confident or you want your puppy to grow into a happy, stress-free adult, counterconditioning and desensitization are powerful learning tools. Combined with positive reinforcement, you can help your pet to grow and learn happily alongside you. 🐾

RULES OF SEPARATION

Keep your animals happy—and safe—when you're away from home

BY JUNO DEMELO

SET UP POTTY BREAKS

Some adult dogs can be left alone for six to eight hours, depending on how chill they are. (High-strung dogs may need more attention.) If you'll be gone longer than that, consider a walker or doggy day care. Even if your pup can go all day without urinating, don't always expect it of him: when a dog consistently holds it in for more than eight hours, he can be at risk of health issues, like urinary tract infections. Indoor potty pads are an option, but dogs need to be trained to use them (and they may become their own kind of bad habit).

CALM THEM DOWN

Your absence can make your pets anxious: dogs with separation anxiety may howl, pace or become destructive. Don't scold them if you arrive home to a chewed-up rug, as this may worsen their anxiety. When they're alone, play soothing music or try a pheromone diffuser (like Adaptil) to help ease their distress. Before you leave, give them plenty of exercise so they're relaxed and sleepy. If these measures don't help after a few weeks, you may want to speak with your vet.

PREOCCUPY THEM

If pets are bored, they may get themselves into trouble. Leave treat-filled toys and puzzles so they stay entertained. They should also have a comfy place to sleep and access to fresh water. An anxious dog may benefit from a quiet or dark place, while a social, interactive dog may want to look out the window. If you don't crate your pets, close doors to bedrooms and bathrooms, or use baby gates to block off trash, food, plants and anything else they might eat or destroy.

ASK FOR HELP

If you think your pet is showing signs of heightened anxiety, including hiding, shaking or depression, check in with your vet. They can help you determine if this is standard separation anxiety or a larger issue (plus the vet can rule out any other underlying causes). Treatment for anxiety may include a combination of training, medications, a certified behaviorist and patience on your part. Often, these types of behaviors can take some time to rectify, so allow ample time for your dog to adjust to being apart.

THE TOOLS

Set up a wide-angle camera in your home linked to your phone to check on your pet remotely. And playing soothing music on a portable speaker may help comfort your dog when you are away. Specific genres, such as classical and reggae, have been shown in clinical testing to be effective in comforting dogs.

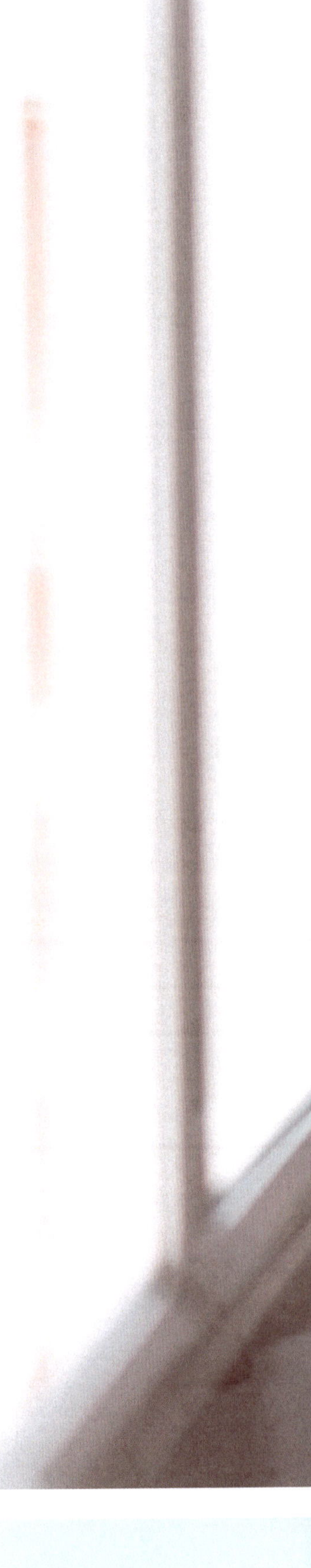

A Plan for a Puppy

Puppies benefit from a regular schedule, just as humans do. It's easy to create an effective one with this quick guide

BY HAYLEE BERGELAND, CPDT-KA, CBCC-KA, RBT

BRINGING HOME a new puppy is exciting . . . and a bit stressful. There are a lot of things to consider, including where your pup will sleep, what he should eat, when to start training and how to get him to go potty outside. But of all the essential things you must plan to do when you add a new canine companion to your family, establishing a regular schedule is one of the most important.

Just like with human babies, dogs need a routine. They need to feel confident in knowing when things will happen, like when they will be fed, when they will go outside and get exercise or when it's just time for play and fun. Providing your dog with a consistent schedule will help them in myriad ways, including potty training, skills training and behavior development. It can seem overwhelming to consider creating an effective schedule for a new pup when you might already struggle with your own, but luckily it's easy to do with this simple guide.

Starting a Schedule for Your Puppy

First things first. Consider your own schedule. When do you eat breakfast? What time do you leave for work in the morning? When do you get home and eat dinner? Your new puppy's schedule should mirror your own. Feed her when you eat, play with her when you get home from work, and give her exercise when you are most likely to do it yourself. But keep in mind that although it may not feel like the end of the world for you to miss a day of fitness or spend too much time on your laptop, it will feel terrible for your pup. Puppies cannot go a day without play sessions or romps around the neighborhood. For your new dog, a daily schedule really does mean Every. Single. Day.

If you find it helpful to have a calendar on your fridge that notes your week's important activities, make one for your puppy, too. You will have to make adjustments in your own routine to accommodate the needs of your new family member, but when you are consistent and deliberate about it the

Although puppy owners may feel guilty for crate training their dog, enclosed spaces help a pup rest and relax.

routine will fall into place easily for both of you.

The sooner you implement a schedule and routine for your puppy the better, as this consistency will help your him adjust to his new life with you.

5 Puppy Daily Routine Elements to Consider

1. FEEDING While puppies grow they eat—a lot—and the amount they eat will change as they age. Most pups under the age of 5 to 6 months need to be fed three meals a day. To make it easy, feed your puppy at the same time you eat breakfast, lunch and dinner. Don't forget to offer lots of clean, fresh water at mealtimes and throughout the day.

2. POTTYING Depending on their age, pups need to potty every one to four hours, with younger puppies needing to go most often.

To help with potty training, puppies should have consistent times throughout the day that are set aside just for going outside. And always remember to let your pup outside the moment you let him out of the crate!

These are the five key times in their day when a dog must be let outside to potty:

- After resting or sleeping
- After play sessions
- After eating and drinking
- Before going to bed or into the crate
- Before and after training sessions

And don't be surprised if your puppy needs to go potty again shortly after he went out. Pups don't always totally eliminate each time they go. If your pup didn't pee when you let him out because he was too busy chasing his buddy or trying to eat the leaves off your bush, then

you will find (much to your chagrin, I bet) that he needs to go as soon as you let him inside. Just be patient and give him plenty of opportunities to get it right.

3. ENRICHMENT AND PLAYTIME Making sure you provide your pup ample enrichment is critical to healthy development. Pups that are denied significant play and enrichment are more likely to have anxiety, to be fearful and lack confidence, to be socially underdeveloped and to have behavioral concerns in adolescence.

Plan out times during your day when your pup gets your undivided attention. Spend time before you leave for work playing with toys or doing some basic training; this will help ease your departure. Leave out interactive toys or puzzles while you are gone to eliminate boredom. The moment you come home each day, go outside and play tug or throw a favorite ball. After dinner take your puppy for a good walk and explore your neighborhood.

Playtimes are great moments that your pup desperately needs, but they should never be overly long or arduous. Think short and sweet: your 3-month-old puppy cannot handle more than 15 to 20 minutes of significant activity at any given time (despite how it might appear) or else she will experience overarousal and overstimulation. Be sure that any time your pup engages in mental and physical stimulation she has the opportunity to rest undisturbed afterward (and get a potty break!).

4. SOCIALIZATION AND LEARNING TIME Of all the things a puppy really needs in order to grow into a happy adult, socialization is probably number one. Socialization is the surest way to prevent behavior issues later on, and it is the thing dog owners tend to overlook. (Avoid this common mistake!)

Canine socialization doesn't mean just taking your dog to the dog park or going to a few puppy classes. Likewise, dog owners must be careful not to flood a new puppy with overwhelming stimulation, as that will only lead to issues later on. Socialization is a systematic process in which you gradually and thoughtfully expose your puppy to the world around him, always at his own pace and always in a positive and safe manner. Understanding how your dog learns is a must, too. (Surprise! They learn just like you!)

Each day should be full of socialization opportunities, which can include teaching basic skills with positive reinforcement and going to puppy training classes, investigating the environment around your home, taking trips to the vet, going on walks on leash, playing around other dogs and new people, and experiencing the sights and sounds of everyday life with you. Again, short and sweet is the key.

5. REST At times, it will feel as if your new puppy will never sleep, and then suddenly he'll seem to do nothing but sleep. As a puppy's body grows and adjusts, so does his sleep schedule. And don't assume that your high-energy puppy doesn't need a nap sometimes!

Pups that do not rest are more likely to turn into little grouchy sharks (your hand will learn this quickly with each nip), so always make sure to listen to your puppy's body language and end playtime before it's just too much.

Plan on quiet times when your pup can rest without distractions from anyone else in the house. Scheduled short naps in the crate or kennel are a good way to get crate training started off on the right paw, ensuring that it becomes a treasured safe space, too.

When it comes to bedtimes, you may find your pup will quickly follow your lead and go to bed when you do. Just remember to always let her potty again right before you both close your eyes for the night.

It will take a few weeks or more for your pup to get used to things and begin to feel at home. The quicker you implement a schedule and stick to a daily routine, the faster your pup will adjust to life with you. 🐾

EASIER VET VISITS

Simple steps to make doctor's appointments more pleasant for you and your animal

BY JUNO DEMELO

NAIL THE TIMELINE

Your pet should get a checkup once a year, though senior animals may need to be seen more frequently. If you'll be transporting your dog in a carrier, help him grow accustomed to it first. Leave it out at least a week in advance (or all the time) and line it with a fluffy towel or blanket to lure him in. This may work for skittish cats too—simply placing a treat in the carrier won't always do the trick. (A cat may also dart out quickly after eating it.) Aim to take pets on regular drives so they don't associate the car only with the vet.

GATHER EVIDENCE

Before your appointment, write down any questions you want to ask in case you forget them in the exam room. Since animals won't always replicate problematic behaviors at the vet, try to catch them on video at home. Note the location of any worrisome lumps or bumps so you can easily find them. (Snip the hair a bit to help you mark the spot.) And if your pet has been given a prescription by another vet, bring the medication to your appointment.

KEEP CALM

Pack special-occasion treats, and withhold a little food the morning of your visit to make them extra enticing. About 15 minutes before you head out, spritz the inside of your car and anything you're bringing to the vet with a pheromone spray, like Adaptil. If you have an aggressive or anxious pet, ask to wait in the car until an exam room opens up. You can also request that your pet be examined in your lap or on the floor. If your pet is still stressed despite your best efforts, talk to your vet about prescribing something to help calm him.

A dog carrier should be large enough for a dog to turn around in easily, and comfortable to curl up in or stretch out when lying down.

How to Nail Housebreaking

Teaching a dog to take potty breaks outside is easy to do with these simple tips

BY HAYLEE BERGELAND, CPDT-KA, CBCC-KA, RBT

TEACHING A DOG OF any age to go potty outside seems like a daunting task for first-time dog owners . . . or anyone who's adding a new four-legged friend to their family. And although it may seem natural to us humans that dogs use the outdoors as a bathroom, it's not coded in doggie DNA to seek out only your grass, and not a rug, to do their business. Dogs need to be taught—with patience, understanding and an enormous amount of positive reinforcement—to go outside.

With these four easy tips you can help any dog decide to use your yard instead of your carpet.

4 Tips to Help Teach Your Dog to Go Potty Outside

Before you get started, ensure your yard or designated outdoor potty area is dog-friendly and that any spaces in your home where your canine student will relax are dog-proofed and suited to their individual needs.

1. USE A BELL I am a huge fan of bell training for potty purposes. Essentially, you teach your dog to ring a bell (attached to a strip or string near the door) whenever she needs to get outside to go potty. I have found great success over the years and continue to use "potty bells" for any new puppy I bring home. The bell can quickly become a clear way for your dog to tell you she needs a potty break.

Training a dog to use a bell is simple with these three steps:

STEP 1: Teach your dog to "nose target" the bell to make it jingle. Hold the bells close to your dog's nose and let him investigate. If he sniffs, touches or boops the bell, mark and reinforce with a favorite treat. Repeat. After several repetitions, move the bell further away so that your dog must take a few steps toward it to touch it.

STEP 2: Once your doggo is touching the bells to get a tasty treat, hang the bells on the doorknob of each door she might use to go outside. Encourage her to touch the bell as it hangs from the doorknob and when she does, mark and reinforce!

STEP 3: Now they need to understand that the bell ringing means the door opens to go outside. The moment your pup touches the bell, open the door, take him outside and give him a treat. If he potties, give him another treat and then immediately go back inside. Repeat this each time you want your pup to go outside, but be sure you are not waiting for him to ring the bell until he is so full he might have an accident while he waits for the door to open.

2. GET THE TIMING RIGHT
Understanding when a dog, especially a young puppy, will need to pee or poop is crucial to successful potty training and will help create a potty-time schedule. Knowing when they might need to go helps you avoid accidents. Look for behaviors like sniffing the ground, pacing, whining or whimpering, jumping on you or following you, becoming more mouthy during play, moving away from you, or quickly running toward another space. These can be indicators a dog needs to pee or poop. There are also times before and after daily events your dog must be let outside.

Dogs need to go outside *after* these key moments:

- After naps or sleeping for any period of time longer than 15 minutes
- After eating
- After drinking
- After a play session
- After a training session
- After a stressful or scary event

Dogs need to go potty *before* these key moments:

- Before going to bed at night (no more than 10 minutes before bedtime!)
- Before being crated or kenneled
- Before a training session or puppy class
- Before friends or family come over for a visit
- Before going inside the vet office

3. REMAIN POSITIVE When dogs are just learning to pee or poop outside you need to constantly provide treats and praise and should never use punishment. Avoid scolding or harsh corrections when your dog has an accident, otherwise you only increase the likelihood she will get better at hiding where she potties inside instead of getting better at peeing outside. Plus, whenever you get upset with your canine you only break the bond you are trying to build. Focus on teaching what to do instead of what not to do.

Offer a tasty treat and praise when your dog goes to the door to let you know he needs to go outside. Each time he uses a potty pad, give lots of good praise, and every time he successfully goes potty outside give a favorite goodie. Make sure you reinforce your dog for making the choice to go potty outdoors consistently, especially during the first few months of training.

Remember that your dog is learning and you are living with a totally different species that doesn't innately understand their toilet should be your grass. It is your job to know when he might need to use the green facilities and it is not your dog's job to teach you. Be patient and keep the whole process laid-back and full of positive

"Remember that your dog is learning and you are living with a totally different species that doesn't innately understand their toilet should be your grass.

Help your pup get used to pee pads by allowing him to sniff and walk on them.

reinforcement opportunities.

4. CLEAN, CLEAN, CLEAN Accidents happen and they are no big deal! Your floor will survive and your dog can learn, with your patience and understanding, that there are better spots to pee. Just make sure to thoroughly clean accident spots, and keep your pup's space clean and tidy and free from items that may have become soiled. Remove a pee pad as soon as it has been used more than once, and launder any bedding or stuffed play toys that have been accidentally soaked.

Things You Definitely Need When You're Teaching Your Dog to Pee Outside

To make your potty training journey a little easier, stock up on these essential items.

PEE PADS Disposable pee pads are a great tool to use when teaching a new pup or an adult dog that needs to relearn potty training in order to go to the bathroom in a designated area. But I often hear dog parents expressing concern over letting their new puppy or rescue use pee pads. They worry their dog will rely on them and generalize the behavior of peeing on the pads to other areas around the home. Thankfully, this is just a myth. Puppies, and any dog learning where to potty, can easily transition from pee pads to the outdoors. Besides, the pads are for temporary use or to help prevent accidents on your flooring. If you are paying close attention

to the potty needs of your dog and getting him outside in time, you will find pee pads are just a stand-in for emergencies until a dog becomes totally potty trained.

CARPET CLEANERS The smell of doggie accidents is no treat for anyone, including your pup, and lingering odors can even entice your dog to use that same spot as a bathroom again. You need to make sure that any soiled areas are thoroughly cleaned. Avoid using any product that contains ammonia. Although it is a common ingredient in many cleaning products, it also happens to be a chemical in urine, and so it only increases the likelihood your dog will urinate in that same spot again.

It is best to use an enzymatic pet stain and odor remover to clean up your furry pal's urine. These cleansers break down the bacteria in the urine and help eliminate the scent, which is crucial to reducing your dog's desire to reuse the same spot for potty business.

BABY GATES When your dog needs to rest, or you are not sure if she is "empty" and may have to potty while you make dinner, use baby gates to safely confine her to a specific space. Block off the entrance to a bedroom with a walk-through gate or make a dog-friendly pen in your living room. This way your canine doesn't have free access to your home, decreasing the chances she will take advantage of your lack of attention and use the carpet in your office as a toilet.

KENNEL OR CRATE Your dog's crate or kennel makes a good resting place after play sessions or while you do chores around the house and can't fully supervise your fur baby. They also work well to help a new pup relax between potty-training breaks, especially if he didn't eliminate when you thought he would. Place the crate in a room where you can still easily see your dog so you can be sure to let him outside to try to potty if you hear him moving about or whimpering. Make sure your dog's crate is the perfect size for him and he is fully comfortable with crate training before you require him to be there for any period of time.

POTTY BELLS Potty bells hung from the door can make potty training a breeze. You will likely want to purchase a set for any door your dog uses to go outside. Make sure the bells are low enough that your dog can easily reach them and is able to signal you with loud rings you can easily hear.

TREATS To encourage a young pup or your new rescue baby to continue to go outside to potty, give her a great reinforcer right when she starts to go. As she begins to tinkle say "Good potty," and as soon as she finishes offer a delicious treat. This makes the whole experience a positive reinforcement opportunity for your canine buddy.

Although successful potty training takes time, plenty of patience and lots of positive reinforcement, it can be a simple process when you are well-prepared. Making sure your canine family member has great potty skills goes a long way toward ensuring both you and your dog are living a happy, relatively clean, stinky-carpet-free life together.

A Dog's Brain

EDITORIAL DIRECTOR Kostya Kennedy
CREATIVE DIRECTOR Gary Stewart
EDITOR Courtney Mifsud
ART DIRECTOR Aaron Morales
PHOTO EDITOR Robert Conway
WRITERS Haylee Bergeland, David Bjerklie, Dan Bova, Austin Cannon, Juno Demelo, Katherine Albro Houpt, Brendan Howard, Emily Joshu, Courtney Mifsud, Holly Pevzner, John Pilley, Lisa Radosta, Kathryn Satterfield
COPY CHIEF Toni Rumore
COPY EDITORS Joel Van Liew, Vanessa Weiman
REPORTER Elizabeth Bland
PHOTO ASSISTANT Charlotte Borge
PRODUCTION DESIGNER Sandra Jurevics
PREMEDIA TRAFFICKING SUPERVISOR Jordan Eischeid
COLOR QUALITY ANALYST Heidi Parcel

MEREDITH PREMIUM PUBLISHING
VICE PRESIDENT & GROUP PUBLISHER Scott Mortimer
VICE PRESIDENT, GROUP EDITORIAL DIRECTOR Stephen Orr
VICE PRESIDENT, MARKETING Jeremy Biloon
DIRECTOR, BRAND MARKETING Jean Kennedy
ASSOCIATE DIRECTOR, BRAND MARKETING Bryan Christian
SENIOR BRAND MANAGER Katherine Barnet

EDITORIAL DIRECTOR Kostya Kennedy
CREATIVE DIRECTOR Gary Stewart
DIRECTOR OF PHOTOGRAPHY Christina Lieberman
EDITORIAL OPERATIONS DIRECTOR Jamie Roth Major
MANAGER, EDITORIAL OPERATIONS Gina Scauzillo

SPECIAL THANKS Brad Beatson, Samantha Lebofsky, Kate Roncinske, Laura Villano

MEREDITH NATIONAL MEDIA GROUP
PRESIDENT Catherine Levene
PRESIDENT, MEREDITH MAGAZINES Doug Olson
PRESIDENT, CONSUMER PRODUCTS Tom Witschi
PRESIDENT, MEREDITH DIGITAL Alysia Borsa
EVP, STRATEGIC & BUSINESS DEVELOPMENT Daphne Kwon

EXECUTIVE VICE PRESIDENTS
CHIEF REVENUE OFFICER Michael Brownstein
DIGITAL SALES Marla Newman
FINANCE Michael Riggs
MARKETING & INTEGRATED COMMUNICATIONS Nancy Weber

SENIOR VICE PRESIDENTS
CONSUMER MARKETING Steve Crowe
CONSUMER REVENUE Andy Wilson
CORPORATE SALES Brian Kightlinger
FOUNDRY 360 Matt Petersen
PRODUCT & TECHNOLOGY Justin Law
RESEARCH SOLUTIONS Britta Cleveland
STRATEGIC PLANNING Amy Third
STRATEGIC SOURCING, NEWSSTAND, PRODUCTION Chuck Howell

VICE PRESIDENTS
BRAND LICENSING Toye Cody and Sondra Newkirk
BUSINESS PLANNING & ANALYSIS Rob Silverstone
FINANCE Chris Susil
STRATEGIC DEVELOPMENT Kelsey Andersen
STRATEGIC PARTNERSHIPS Alicia Cervini

VICE PRESIDENT, GROUP EDITORIAL DIRECTOR Stephen Orr
CHIEF DIGITAL CONTENT OFFICER Amanda Dameron
DIRECTOR, EDITORIAL OPERATIONS & FINANCE Greg Kayko

MEREDITH CORPORATION
CHAIRMAN & CHIEF EXECUTIVE OFFICER Tom Harty
CHIEF FINANCIAL OFFICER Jason Frierott
CHIEF DEVELOPMENT OFFICER John Zieser
PRESIDENT, MEREDITH LOCAL MEDIA GROUP Patrick McCreery
SENIOR VICE PRESIDENT, HUMAN RESOURCES Dina Nathanson
SENIOR VICE PRESIDENT, CHIEF COMMUNICATIONS OFFICER Erica Jensen

VICE CHAIRMAN Mell Meredith Frazier

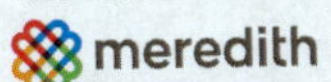

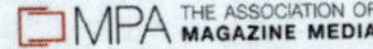

Published by Meredith Corporation
225 Liberty Street • New York, NY 10281

Printed in the USA.

CREDITS

FRONT COVER abezikus/iStock/Getty Images

BACK COVER (clockwise from top) fcscafeine/iStock/Getty Images; alexei_tm/iStock/Getty Images; LWA/Stone RF/Getty Images

P. 1 Penny Britt/iStock/Getty Images
PP. 2–3 (clockwise from left) Image Source/Photodisc/Getty Images; Silk and Salt Images/Moment/Getty Images; Elena Duvernay/EyeEm/Getty Images; Woraphon Nusen/EyeEm/Getty Images
PP. 4–5 4FR/E+/Getty Images
P. 6 SPUTNIK/Alamy
P. 7 Andalou Agency/Getty Images
P. 8 Micah Youello/E+/Getty Images
P. 9 Cavan Images/Getty Images
PP. 10–11 Sadeugra/E+/Getty Images
PP. 12–13 Eniko Kubinyi/AFP/Getty Images
P. 14 Rebecca Nelson/Photodisc/Getty Images
P. 17 Raymond McCrea Jones/Redux
P. 18 Courtesy of Federico Rossano
P. 20 Chrisitina Reichl Photography/Moment/Getty Images
PP. 22–29 Sebastien Micke/Paris Match/Getty Images (4)
PP. 30–31 Justin Paget/DigitalVision/Getty Images
PP. 32–33 E+/Getty Images
P. 35 Johny87/iStock/Getty Images
P. 36 twomeows/Moment/Getty Images
PP. 38–39 Tim Macpherson/Cultura/Getty Images
PP. 40–41 Hans Surfer/Moment/Getty Images
P. 43 juhy13/E+/Getty Images
PP. 44–45 Cavan Images/Getty Images
P. 47 Rebecca Nelson/Image Source/Getty Images
P. 48 otsphoto/Shutterstock
P. 51 Photoboyko/iStock/Getty Images
P. 52 Renphoto/E+/Getty Images
P. 55 monicapisaphotography/Moment/Getty Images
PP. 56–57 iStock/Getty Images
P. 59 Cultura/Getty Images
P. 60 Marija Kovac/Stocksy
PP. 62–63 alexei_tm/iStock/Getty Images
P. 65 Natalia Fedosova/Shutterstock
PP. 66–67 Gary Martin/iStock/Getty Images
PP. 68–69 Inna Skaldutska/Getty Images
PP. 70–71 Alex Griffin/E+/Getty Images
PP. 72–73 alexei_tm/iStock/Getty Images
P. 75 Bettmann/Getty Images
P. 76 Rich Legg/E+/Getty Images
PP. 78–79 Annette Birkenfeld/E+/Getty Images
PP. 80–81 Andrey Popov/iStock/Getty Images
PP. 82–83 Eva Blanco/iStock/Getty Images
PP. 84–85 Stefan Cristian Cioata/Moment/Getty Images
PP. 86–87 Searsie/E+/Getty Images
PP. 88–89 (from left) Reshetnikov_art/Shutterstock; Xixinxing/Getty Images
PP. 90–91 Aitor Diago/Moment/Getty images
P. 93 E+/Getty Images
P. 94 Nicky Lloyd/E+/Getty Images
P. 95 Esther Moreno/EyeEm/Getty images
P. 96 Brat Co/Stocksy

WATCH THE WAG

Tail movements can signal specific feelings and provide insight into a dog's mind

DOGS COMMUNICATE WHAT THEY'RE THINKING and feeling through body language, such as tail wagging. Learn how to pick up on their cues to enrich your relationship and keep both you and your pet safe.

Signaling Happiness: Tail is level with back or slightly above or below back and wagging. (If your dog has a curly or docked tail, evaluate based on what's normal for your dog.)

Signaling Curiosity: Tail is held straight out horizontally in a neutral position while taking in new information.

Signs of Stress: Tail is high above back or tucked and wagging. If your dog displays stressed-out symptoms, identify the trigger, remove him from the situation, or resolve the issue. Use a calm, neutral tone of voice when speaking and offer high-value rewards to help divert his attention.

Made in the USA
Monee, IL
13 April 2024